I'm Going to College—*Not You!*

I'm Going to College—
Not You!

Surviving the College Search with Your Child

·······

Edited by
Jennifer Delahunty

ST. MARTIN'S GRIFFIN
NEW YORK

www.stmartins.com

Book design by Level C

Library of Congress Cataloging-in-Publication Data

I'm going to college—not you! : surviving the college search with your child / edited by Jennifer Delahunty. — 1st ed.
    p. cm.
  ISBN 978-0-312-60729-6
  1. College choice—United States.   2. Universities and colleges—United States.   3. Education, Higher—Aims and objectives.   I. Delahunty, Jennifer.
  LB2350.5.I6 2010
  378.1'98—dc22

                                                              2010014926

First Edition: September 2010

10 9 8 7 6 5 4 3 2 1

For Emma and Maddie . . .
my favorite college students, always.

Contents

Acknowledgments   xi

Introduction   1

Part 1
Where It All Begins

An Unsentimental Education   13
Neal Pollack

A Cautionary Tale   20
Christine VanDeVelde

Personal Statement   25
Wendy MacLeod

Part 2
From the Outsiders

**How to Get into College Without
Really Trying**   31
Gail Hudson

The Age of Reasons 46

Joe Queenan

Application Madness 51

Anne C. Roark

A Piece of Cake 70

Jan Brogán

Part 3
From the Insiders

Impersonating Wallpaper

The Dean's Daughter Speaks 81

Jennifer Delahunty and Emma Britz

A Life of Too Much 91

Lisa Gates

The Kids Are Alright 100

(With Apologies to The Who)

Debra Shaver

Let It/Them Be 103

(With or Without Apologies to The Beatles),

or How *Not* to Spend Your Child's Summer Vacation

Katherine Sillin

Part 4
From a Mother's Perspective

The Deep Pool   113
Anna Quindlen

When Love Gets in the Way   116
Jane Hamilton

Hooked   121
Laurie Kutchins

Our Quixotic Quests for Utopia U   129
Anna Duke Reach

Part 5
From a Father's Perspective

Market Lambs and Chaos Warriors   137
Dan Laskin

Flowers Will Grow   145
Sean Callaway

The Worst of Times, the Best of Times   154
The Scholar-Athlete Applies to College
David Latt

From the Belly of the Whale   164
David H. Lynn

Where the Chips Fall   171
Scott Sadil

Part 6
Road Trippin'

The Most Difficult Year to Get into College in the History of the World
Excerpts from "The Neurotic Parent" Blog   181
The Neurotic Parent

Laundry, Lost Luggage, and
Lord of the Rings   216
Lisa K. Winkler

Sound Tracks   223
Joy Horowitz

Part 7
A User's Guide for Parents

Love in the Time of College Angst   231
S. X. Rosenstock

Wait Outside   244
Sarah Kahrl

Sophie, Real and Imagined   251
Ellen Waterston

T-minus Thirteen Minutes and
Forty-one Seconds   258
Steve Thomas

About the Contributors   265
Copyright Acknowledgments   275

Acknowledgments

This book was conceived in the company of friends and is born in their company as well. Many of the authors were or have become good friends in the course of collecting these essays. I can't imagine a better cast of writing companions.

My agent, Agnes Birnbaum, has been a rare amalgam of cheerleader, taskmaster, and wizard. Without her, this book never would have been. I'm so glad you're on my side, Agnes.

Editor Michelle Richter is the kind of person who always finds the four-leaf clover without looking too hard. Her humor, professionalism, and enthusiasm kept the project going; her keen sensibilities and book-smart intelligence made the manuscript as strong as it could be. *Molte grazie,* Michelle, to you and St. Martin's.

I'm also deeply grateful to President Georgia Nugent and the trustees of Kenyon College for giving me three critical things: encouragement, permission to speak the truth (even when it was difficult), and time to devote to this manuscript. To the Kenyon admissions and financial aid staffs, and in particular Kim Totman, Darryl Uy, and Bev Morse: a huge thumbs-up. Your application files correctly indicate that you are all A-rated colleagues and friends.

To Betsy Anderson: Thanks for sharing your golden

Rolodex of writer-friends who all came through beautifully, just as you said they would.

To Steve Thomas: Thanks for letting me add skin and bone to this idea while in residence at 21 Water Street. (It's a good thing nothing is ever happening at the Yellow House.) You'll never know how much it means to me that you believed in this book and my ability to make it happen.

To my daughters: How embarrassing this all was for you, to have your mother write about your college searches and tell your stories in front of thousands of people. Thank you for letting me put you on the page and for gracefully smiling through it all. Feel free to write your books about me now. To my parents: Thanks for teaching me the value and magic of words—and, oh yes, for making sure I went off to college.

And finally, to the many students and parents who have, over the years, generously allowed me to counsel and observe them as they navigated the labyrinth of college choice: my heartfelt gratitude.

Introduction

I raised my two daughters with a lot of help from other parents. They taught me how to mix cereal with mashed bananas, how to seduce a recalcitrant two-year-old into napping alone in a big bed, how to endure the disrespectful lip of a headstrong middle-schooler. During my daughters' teenage years, my most valued parental guide was Julie, whose two teenagers had been giving her a run for her money. "If it has testosterone and tires, it spells trouble," was the refrigerator magnet I bought her when her son wrecked his first car. We laughed and commiserated frequently over the challenges of raising our manipulative and moody, magical and mysterious teenagers.

I was sitting on Julie's couch a few years back, and she handed me a collection of essays about raising teenagers called *I Wanna Be Sedated.* We read these essays aloud to each other and laughed and cried and exclaimed over the truths contained therein. When I read Gail Hudson's essay, "How to Get into College Without Really Trying" (page 31), a thought balloon blossomed above my middle-aged head. What about an anthology of essays by parents about the college search process? It seemed like an idea ripe for picking. I imagined a collection that included insiders—those admissions professionals, like me, who knew too much—as well as outsiders—those who applied to college twenty-five years ago when the process was as easy as signing up to join the YMCA. I imagined a book that was not a "how to" (too many books of that ilk already exist) but, rather, a "how to survive" this process if you're a parent.

Well, here is that book—thanks to some really wonderful writers, and an agent and editor who believed in the concept.

Raise the topic of college choice in any setting—a dinner party, a book club meeting, the supermarket line—and you'll find yourself in the middle of a lively conversation. Trust me. It happens every time I am forced to tell my seatmate on an airplane what I do for a living. "Really, an admissions dean? My son is looking at Universal U and Impenetrable Ivy and . . ." And we're off and running.

I have those conversations on planes because I am often flying off to speak at gatherings of parents and students who are in the midst of the college search process. My talks are best received when I share my perspective as both a dean *and* as a parent of teenagers traveling through the fraught gauntlet of college choice. The merging of the personal and the professional infuses the experience with more juice. And I have dozens of such stories to share.

My two daughters had had fairly straightforward college searches, each with a surprise ending. My oldest daughter had done an aggressive college search on both coasts and then chose—to my chagrin and delight—to stay close to home for college. My youngest daughter, the more difficult but less assured one, had a way of keeping me not just at arm's length during the process but at more than a semi-truck length away. One night over dinner during her senior year, when I once again brought up the content of her Common Application essay, she slammed her spoon down on the table and shouted at me, "All you talk about is college and preventing pregnancy."

"You're seventeen years old and a senior in high school. What else is there to talk about?" I said, my parental filter clearly malfunctioning.

And that's when I realized that this whole last dance of parenting turns all of us—no matter how smart or experienced—into stumbling idiots. Why?

College choice has become the crucible of anxiety for millions of parents and students across the country. Acceptance of a son or daughter by a top college, as defined by the nebulous prestige mongers, has become the coin of the realm, the ultimate "good parenting" seal of approval. The better the bumper sticker, the better the parent, right? Every cocktail party from Manhattan to Monterey includes conversations about college tours, SAT tutors, summer "enrichment" programs, and ultimately, application and acceptance lists. Parents with juniors and seniors in high school are obsessed with finding the key that will open the lock to just the right college. A recent Nielsen poll placed "children's education" on par with adult worries about their own health. Only job security, work/life balance, and the economy rated higher on adult Americans' "worry meter."

It's hard to avoid the topic. Open any American newspaper or magazine today and you'll find a story about colleges: high tuition, low selectivity, excessive luxuries, a deficit of available classes. Both the media and the masses are obsessed with college choice. While Americans expect fairness and logic to prevail, admissions decisions can appear to be random if not downright whimsical. A meritocracy it is not. The mysterious black box of college admissions continues to frustrate and infuriate the public.

With so much uncertainty about why some students get in and others don't, college choice has become a big business. More than two million students enter college each year, and at present, three major related industries are together generating a billion dollars annually: (1) test preparation (e.g., Kaplan and the Princeton Review), (2) testing agencies themselves (e.g., College Board and ACT), and (3) independent counselors who charge up to $25,000 per student to "get your child into the college of their dreams." Clearly, someone needs to tell this generation of students and parents to *chill*.

Parental expectations for college attainment run headlong into a very stark reality. Today's college admissions landscape is defined by excessive competition, rampant fear, ignorance, unpredictability, and vexing behavior—on the part of the prospective college student, on the part of the parents, and, especially, on the part of the colleges themselves. Competition for top spots is fierce: The largest high school graduating class in American history will graduate in the 2008–2012 timeframe (demographers differ on the precise year). The prolific baby boomers have given birth to a boomlette—or *echo boom*—of aspiring college students. In fact, there are 800,000 more students attending college today in America than there were twenty years ago. There are simply *not* 800,000 more seats.

Allow me to play that out for you in terms of a young person's chances of being admitted to one of the top twenty-five universities or one of the top twenty-five liberal arts colleges in the country, according to *U.S. News & World Report.* And as we know, *U.S. News & World Report* isn't the definitive way to measure quality or the best college—but for purposes of this exercise, let's use that metric.

There are approximately 42,000 spots in the freshman class at the top twenty-five universities and about 12,000 spots in the freshman class at the top twenty-five liberal arts colleges, for a total of 54,000 spots in all. Two million high school students will matriculate in college in 2009. If you do the math, there are spaces at the top twenty-five universities and top twenty-five liberal arts colleges for *only 2.9 percent* of the college-bound population. That's what you call hefty competition. Drill down deeper: More than 2,500 of Harvard's 27,462 applicants scored a perfect 800 on the SAT critical reading test, and 3,300 had 800 scores on the SAT math exam. More than 3,300 were ranked first in their high school class. "Unattainable" is not a word that this generation of parents is accustomed to hearing—especially when it comes to their children.

That's where the craziness begins. "The worst part [of the college admissions process] is dealing with the frenzied parents who seem to go temporarily insane while marketing their children as if they were products," said Ted O'Neill, former dean of admissions, University of Chicago. "Parents are setting an example of bad behavior by seeking untoward advantages and wanting things for their child which are not in his or her best interest."

And why wouldn't we boomers make asses of ourselves over all of this? The generational researchers Howe and Strauss have pointed out that boomer parents want it all for their sons and daughters—their sound track has been a combination of personal fulfillment (cue "Age of Aquarius") *and* financial success (cue the O'Jays' "For the Love of Money"). And what better first step than getting into the "right" college, where you'll meet the "right" friends and, if you're lucky, the "right" life partner. And when you look at the access to a network of highly placed professionals, admission to a top college becomes the Insta-Pass to the fast track in the mind of many a parent.

Add the stress of attaining the right offer of admission to the price tag and you have a truly potent cocktail of anxiety. The cost of a private college has climbed to the nose-bleed zone—circa $200,000. But when you consider that even a school such as SUNY (State University of New York) will cost more than $100,000 if living on campus, then you might think a 100-percent surcharge for a smaller, more personal private college is a bargain.

Sure, there are millions of dollars of financial aid out there, but the amount a family is eligible for isn't known up front. What other product or service is there on the market that you don't know what it's going to cost until four weeks before you have to make a major purchasing decision? That's how financial aid works at many of the selective liberal arts colleges—you get your admissions decision and financial aid package sometime in late March or early April and then you have to make your choice by May 1. More B.S. than B.A., eh? Talk about a formula for explosive family dinner conversations.

Indeed, college choice often comes at the apex of parent-child conflict, when teens are striking out for independence and parents are grasping for control. How can parents help a son or daughter going through this process—a tender and fraught experience—when he or she prevents you from entering his or her room? The essays in this collection address the tightrope parents must walk between "control freak" and "friend."

The conflict can ignite right from the beginning. Parents and students have to be in agreement on "the list," and students today apply at ten to twelve schools, with some applying to as many as twenty. And if a child's application list differs dramatically from the parents' list, the parents shooting high and the student aiming for independence from parental expectations, a major domestic war can break out. Add high school guidance counselors or independent counselors, siblings, friends, neighbors, and anyone else who encounters a high school senior and you have a "too many cooks spoil the broth" scenario. And by the time the student actually has to select where they will spend the next four years—at some point in the spring of the senior year—a full-blown internecine nuclear conflict can erupt in the family room.

College is often the first adult choice a younger person will make, even though the stakes are high and the experience life-defining. And this is where the friction and confusion come in: After seventeen years of tucking their babies in at night, washing soccer shorts, and signing permits for class trips, parents of college-going students find themselves in a confounding situation. What is the right stance to take? How can a parent be helpful but not too interfering? How can a parent resist the path of "helicopter parent" and instead be more of, say, a "booster rocket"? How does one provide college guidance to a son who wants only to become a rock star or a daughter who believes she's the next Hollywood ingenue?

What do you do when your child isn't typical "college mate-rial"? And most important, how does one sleep for the eighteen to twenty-four months in which our children are enduring this process?

The essays in this book—comforting, insightful, amusing, poignant—address these questions, and many others, through personal, hard-won experience. The authors are all sensitive to protecting the privacy of their sons and daughters while offering helpful guidance and humor to fellow parents. Every writer-parent's experience is a little different and there are no formulae for happy endings. Whatever your compunction, furniture rearrangement or tongue biting, you'll find that every writer in this collection finds a coping mechanism for getting through the experience. Not unlike labor and deliv-ery, this process does end at some point, the essayists assure us, and eventually your son or daughter will walk off into the sunset with a college or university name—though probably not the one you expected—on their T-shirt.

I do hope readers will find this collection of essays a kind of counselor and a friend to keep by the bedside when worry-ing about deadlines, essays, and, ultimately, the decision as to where your child will spend the four (or five or six) years it will take to earn a college degree. And, as many of the enclosed essays bear out, if you prepare for a nonlinear, wild ride—one akin to that of Mr. Toad—it will all work out in the end and your son or daughter will land just where he or she should. And maybe, just maybe, if you play your cards right, you'll have a better, deeper, and more nuanced understanding of your child, yourself, and your relationship with him or her.

And whichever college he or she attends will, as it should, matter much less than the quality of the relationship that evolved between the two of you as you traveled the long and winding road toward college.

Part 1

. . . .

Where It All Begins

An Unsentimental Education

....

Neal Pollack

Forty-eight hours after my son's birth, my mother gazed upon the red, wrinkled, gassy form of her first grandchild and said, almost like an incantation:

"Harvard . . . Princeton . . . Yale . . ."

Just like that, before he'd even pooped for the first time, someone had placed obnoxiously unrealistic educational expectations upon Elijah's head. But when you come from a family where everyone went to college and more than one member has multiple Ivy League graduate degrees, it shouldn't come as a surprise to hear "boola boola," or some equally annoying equivalent, in the maternity ward. Note that Grandma didn't wish the boy (who, until very recently, had been a fetus with limited educational prospects) health, happiness, or prosperity. His getting into an elite private university would provide all that automatically. It was the secular equivalent of the king-dom of heaven.

It's probably a good idea for *any* kid to attend college, unless that child is LeBron James, Kobe Bryant, or maybe Taylor

Swift, people who got their tickets punched in other ways. If Elijah were to be accepted, someday, to Harvard, Princeton, or Yale, I'd *kvell* off my remaining hair. I'd also immediately begin to panic at the prospect of what the resulting debt would mean for his parents, a freelance writer and a painter with limited commercial prospects. If college were what the boy really wanted, I'd move mountains, or at least climb them, to make it happen. But my own experience leads me to want him to want more. Somewhat to my surprise, I've found myself thinking differently.

"College ain't so great, kid," I said in that hospital room, in response to my mother. "Life's about more than that."

"I wish you'd come to that conclusion before I borrowed a hundred grand to send you to Northwestern," Mom said.

She had me there.

. . . .

WITH THE EXCEPTION of 1983, which I mostly spent in the bathroom masturbating, my entire childhood revolved around one mission: getting into college. From age seven on, whenever I found myself having to fill out one of those "goal sheets" that seem to appear in front of you with disturbing regularity when you're in school, I always wrote, as my primary ambition: "To get into the university of my choosing." I also wanted to be a writer, but I thought you couldn't possibly become a writer if you didn't go to college. To me, they meant the exact same thing.

While kids around me were busy idolizing Axl Rose, Dan Marino, and Jesus Christ, I found myself hero-worshiping Alex P. Keaton, the character played by Michael J. Fox on

Family Ties. It wasn't Alex's bowdlerized Reagan-era politics that attracted me, but rather, the fact that he shared my single-minded obsession with getting into college. Above all else, he was an achiever, a *good student.* College, sweet college, sat waiting for him at the end of the Principal's List rainbow. That was where achievers achieved, where great minds thought alike, where the seeds of greatness germinated. When I saw *Back to School* at the Paradise Valley Mall in 1986, and Rodney Dangerfield exclaimed to the skies, "I'm goin' to college! I'm goin' to college! I'm goin' to college!" I thought, *Yes, yes, yes!* Then I found myself disappointed that he wasted his college experience on throwing parties and hiring Oingo Boingo as the headliner. College, in my goal-diseased mind, was for studying and getting ahead, not fun.

In high school, I signed up for clubs that I didn't like, ran for student council offices that I didn't care about, and took AP classes in subjects that didn't interest me. My ambitions were entirely focused. Not only was I going to get into the school of my choosing, I was going to get into the *journalism* school of my choosing. The desire to go to college got mixed up with professional ambition. By age fifteen, I'd become a self-righteous rocket of careerist obnoxiousness. My summers were spent at radio stations and newspapers, padding my résumé. I went to high school newspaper conferences, and became a reporter for the teen page of the now-long-defunct *Phoenix Gazette.* While members of my circle who actually knew how to be teenagers were off smoking pot and listening to decent music, I read elitist memoirs by now-forgotten *New York Times* editors, and thought that someday, I, too, would be a boring, cosseted, Upper East Side twit.

So when it came time to get into college, I knew where I wanted to go: Northwestern University's Medill School of Journalism, which had the best undergraduate journalism school in the country. I gathered my recommendation letters, traveled to Chicago, did my interview, and wrote my dopey essays with blind confidence. And then, one afternoon, I came home from school, opened the mailbox, and there was my early acceptance. I went inside, sat on the toilet, read it over and over again, and whooped with joy. I started making phone calls to tell everyone the glorious news.

I was goin' to college, I was goin' to college, I was goin' to college!

· · · · · · ·

EIGHT MONTHS LATER, I sat in a dark corner of my dorm room, my nuts tingling from excessive Everclear consumption, sobbing into my futon chair as the resident assistant rubbed my back, whispering useless platitudes. My experience at college had been thus: The guys in the room next door mocked me because I'd never heard the Public Enemy album. Then, for some reason, I rushed fraternity row so successfully that I actually got offers from two houses. But I wasn't a frat guy. I was a sensitive artist, or at least a journalist with an artistic side. This wasn't what I'd wanted. If anything, college seemed even more cliquish than high school, and there was no escape.

"MY LIFE IS A LIE!" I moaned.

Classes hadn't yet started.

From there, my attitude didn't improve much. Much of my freshman year, I was drunk and depressed, not understanding, for some reason, that alcohol actually caused depression. My sophomore year was even worse. I spent many hours walking the frozen, windswept shores of Lake Michigan and contemplating suicide, or at least dropping out. Meanwhile, I made some friends, helped start a magazine, did some okay work, drove into the city and saw some awesome midnight movies, and went to a really great Pogues concert in 1989. But that wasn't what I'd expected from college. When I'd begun, I was happy and enthusiastic, full of school and dorm spirit, ready to take on the world. By my senior year, I was skipping classes in favor of dropping acid with punk rockers from Louisville.

The journalism school got me an internship at a restaurant trade magazine in Des Plaines, and then I saw what the mainstream working world was really like: boring and full of early risers. I wrote some columns for the school newspaper to this effect, which didn't endear me to the dean's office. There would be no honor roll for me at Medill. I'd spent my whole life trying to get into college, and I spent my whole time in college trying to get out.

Somehow, I graduated a semester early, and I decided to cash in my extra time by taking a cross-country trip on Amtrak. I slept for a few weeks on a friend's couch in Bend, Oregon, and a few more weeks in a friend's garage in San Diego. There were many stoned, meaningless days, hours in coffeehouses playing backgammon, conversations with weirdos in the dining car. With the exception of a couple of mopey days where I watched an old grade-school friend have a Christian identity crisis in an on-campus apartment at Azusa Pacific University, I had more fun, and gathered more experiences, than I did in any one year of college.

Then I took the train back to Chicago to go through my graduation ceremony, even though I'd graduated in my mind long before. My grandmother wanted to see me in the cap and gown. These kinds of milestones matter in my family. So I got stoned and waved a plastic dinosaur bone around while Dick Gephardt motivated us, and then moved forward to a summer of shrooming and playing pickup basketball. Grandma would have been so proud if she'd known.

. . . .

ALL THAT BILE aside, the fact that I went to college enriched my life in many ways. I took classes from at least two excellent writing teachers whose influence I draw upon even now. Some of my closest, and most loyal, friends come from that time. And it certainly hasn't hurt my career. I made connections that helped a lot. One of my J-school teachers was the former managing editor of the *Chicago Reader*, where I ended up working as a staff writer for six happy years in the 1990s. From time to time, other people who I went to school with appear to give me a professional boost. There are reasons why you go to school, for sure. My naïve mistake was in believing it would be the key to my eternal happiness.

My son is seven now, and he and his friends have just begun talking about college. Their discussions usually involve two schools: UCLA, because they've taken some field trips there, and Barnett College, otherwise known as the place where Indiana Jones teaches. When Elijah talks about going to college, his ambitions mostly seem to be about wanting to learn a lot of different languages so that he can talk to people when he goes on archeological digs between semesters. In other words, he wants to be Indiana Jones.

This is a laudable goal, in many respects. Indiana Jones, though fictional, has an interesting life and is apparently something close to immortal. However, I want to remind my son, Indy did a lot more in his youth than just go to college. If you watch old episodes of *The Young Indiana Jones Chronicles*, which Elijah doesn't because there's not enough action, you'll see that Indy, in addition to being well educated, also drove an ambulance in World War I, fought Dracula, and got involved in a lot of wacky old Hollywood intrigue, while traveling the world and meeting famous historical figures. He did a lot more with his youth than just go to college. But *I* didn't, and it's one of my major regrets. My determination to get into the university of my choosing made the early part of my life kind of boring. So now I want to bestow the following wisdom unto my son: Harvard, Princeton, Yale, sure. But do something else, too.

A Cautionary Tale

·······

Christine VanDeVelde

I will share with you the mantra that helped me through the college admission years: "The Unabomber went to Harvard." Remember this. It works much better than "Om." And notice I said "years" because in hypercompetitive Silicon Valley, where I live, the quest for the punched ticket to an undergraduate degree starts early.

Around here, if you have an eleven-year-old applying to middle school, the accepted wisdom is that it is harder to get a seat in the incoming sixth grade of a private school than an acceptance letter from Yale. Despite the fact that I am a journalist—inquiring mind and all—I swallowed this whole. As a well-known psychiatrist once said to me, "All parents are amateurs." Guilty as charged.

And so it was that when my daughter applied to private schools for sixth grade, I got a preview of what college admission frenzy looks like. Although I didn't know it at the time, it turned out to be a lucky lesson. Now it can be a cautionary tale. The truth is that, like the most popular colleges, the private schools in Silicon Valley don't have a seat for everyone who wants one. There isn't the tradition here of private schooling found in the East, because, historically, California public schools provided a terrific education for their students. But over the last thirty years, as problems have beset that system, people fled into the few private schools we have. Today, the admittance rate at most Bay Area private schools is about 25 percent—much like the acceptance rate of, for example, University of Chicago, Duke, Davidson, Johns Hopkins, and Vassar in recent years.

These are market conditions tailor-made to ramp up anxiety and hyperbole. Just like the conceit that there are only eight good colleges in America—no need to name names, you know who they are—there is plenty of hyperbole for the parents of preteens to pass around, too. The principal at my daughter's elementary school called it "broccoli talk"—the "intelligence" shared over the cruciferous bin at the grocery store. For example, did you know that there are one hundred applications for every seat at School X? And parents have to make a six-figure donation before their child is even admitted at School Y—I saw it in the school's annual report! If you're not a wealthy venture capitalist, a movie star, a San Francisco 49er, a *somebody*, your child doesn't stand a chance.

Now, middle school admissions are unlike college in an important way. Colleges are admitting young adults. Middle schools are actually admitting families and have an interest in vetting them to make sure they buy into the school's vision and mission statement. Even so, every once in a while they make a mistake and an atheist pops up at the Episcopal school who spends the next five years advocating to get rid of Secret Santa and the Christmas pageant.

So maybe I can be forgiven somewhat for what happened.

As we made the rounds from open house to open house,

made sure our daughter got a good night's sleep before she "shadowed" at prospective schools, and filled out the applications that had more questions for us than they did for her— *Please describe how you see yourself becoming involved in our community*—I made the mistake then and there that most parents wait to make until the college admission dance begins. It became all about me.

And by the end of the process, I had picked out the perfect school for myself—I mean, my daughter. The problem was she had picked out a perfect school, too, and it wasn't the one I had set my sights on.

What's worse, *my* school wait-listed her. Her school sent a letter filled with glitter and sparkly stars and a note penned on the bottom saying, "You must be so proud. Roark is a gem!" But that didn't deter me. For thirty-six hours after the notifications arrived, I pouted and plotted and phoned everyone I knew at *my* school for advice. In the meantime, of course, no one was celebrating my daughter's acceptance to *her* school. Finally, my dear husband, with narrowed eyes and gritted teeth, hissed at me, "Do not ruin this for her."

It was an epiphany. I'll never forget the look on his face. Or hers—when I finally looked at her. To this day, it breaks my heart that I stole that celebratory moment from her.

But the good thing that came from it was that when it came time to look at colleges, I had already learned to pull my personal stake out of her heart. I had no horse in that race. But I still had a *parental* stake in the decision.

This time I wanted her to get what *she* wanted—but it would only be hers if she did it on her own. Now I'm sure Silicon Valley is like a lot of places in America. But I have never seen a place where people were so obsessed with bench-marks and where individuals so identified with institutions. When I moved here from the Midwest twenty years ago, I thought all these Stanford people should get over themselves. They didn't even have a good football team. Can you say "Cornhuskers"? Nevertheless, the competitiveness and trophy-hunting are relentless here.

The playwright Wendy Wasserstein dubbed it "the Mommy Olympics"—where the broccoli talk convinces you that "all of the two-year-olds are sleeping well enough to take their SATs tomorrow." In this competition, there is proficiency in potty training, trial runs through the child's ace T-ball ath-leticism and early fluency in Mandarin, heats in how many AP courses can be racked up, the race to perfect SAT II scores, and ultimately the gold medal for the fat envelope from the right college. The bragging, the one-upmanship disguised as "advice," the lobbying for preferential treatment, and the search for the shrewdest, fastest inside track . . . OMG! It doesn't leave a lot of bandwidth for discovering what your kids want to do with their lives.

So when it came time for my daughter to apply to college, through an act of will and the memory of her face when she was eleven, I worked at keeping *my* self-worth and status out of the process. But privately I second-guessed myself, wonder-ing whether I was doing the right thing. Why wouldn't I? If everybody else is hiring consultants to quarterback their child's college applications, what will happen to my darling daughter's, pored over and penned on her own? If my daugh-ter decides she doesn't really want to take AP bio and opts out of that class, how does she stack up against the kid who slogs through it, tutored every Tuesday and Thursday? If she doesn't medal in the Mommy Olympics, how will she ever get into one of those eight colleges!?

And this is where my mantra came in. Every time a parent divulged their kid's test scores (though, of course, they didn't want to brag) or cautioned me about my daughter's choices when it came to how she spent her free time (the big risk being that she had any), or made sure I knew how many Ivies their child was applying to (most of them, most of the time), I chanted. *The Unabomber went to Harvard. The Unabomber went to Harvard.*

Nothing against Harvard . . . truly. But it reminded me that Mother doesn't always know best, that where my daughter went to school was not the sole determinant of future success, that there is no right answer. What mattered was that my daughter was healthy. She was happy. She could do this. She applied early decision to a school that she chose because she knew that when she walked across the quad every day she would see people that she knew, and where, she said to me, "By the time I graduate, I will *own* this place."

In the meantime, though, the parental stake I still had in her college search got lodged in my skull. I wanted her to get what she wanted and I guess I wanted it bad. In the ten days leading up to the snail-mail notification of her acceptance, I got a headache that wouldn't go away. I told my husband I must have hurt my neck. I made an appointment with the chiropractor, then with a masseuse. Miraculously, the day my daughter opened her acceptance letter, the headache went away. Just in time for us to celebrate. I was proud of her. And that's so much better than being proud of me.

Personal Statement

. . . .

Wendy MacLeod

*P*lease God, let me in. Just let me *in*. Get my mother off
my *back*.

I can't think of any "significant experiences, achievements,
or risks taken" because *nothing's ever happened to me*. I abandoned my diary because I was even boring myself. I would
literally write the words "Dear Diary" and begin to nod off!
But you have it in your power to *make* something happen to
me. Send me the letter, the fat one with the information on
deposits, roommate assignments, and bicycle storage. Take a
chance on me, and I'm sure I'll do something *eventually*.

And I can't possibly write about "encountering adversity,"
because the worst adversity I've faced so far was the really bad
pimple that emerged on my nose the day of the spring mad-
rigal concert. But isn't that a good thing? Am I to be punished
for a comfortable, middle-class existence? (P.S. The pimple
was at the very end of my nose so I looked like the Wicked
Witch of the West minus the black, the broom, and the little
dog.)

Describe my "values, goals, experiences, talents, style." I
mean, how long have you got? (Just kidding.) I will only say

that, unlike my classmates, I never settled for wearing a hoodie, jeans, and Adidas. We don't have to look at ourselves, other people have to look at us, so isn't it an act of charity to dress stylishly? In this regard, I benefit from the employee discount at Abercrombie & Fitch where I work part time. (Please note work ethic. Most of my friends don't even *have* jobs. They're all like: "Why do you have a job? Wouldn't it be more fun *not* to have a job?")

As far as a person who has had a significant influence on me, that would probably be my mother, but in this case, *significant* does not mean *good*. Every time she comes home from a dinner party, she reminds me that so-and-so is training to be a wilderness guide in Alaska, or that someone is working on an organic farm in Morocco or doing *dressage*. Not to throw myself a pity party, but I've been running myself ragged with extracurricular activities, which my mother practically *mandated*. When I expressed a *slight* reluctance to continue with Debate Club, she was all like, "Go ahead. Quit. You can always go to cosmetology school." Har-de-har-har.

You let Dennis Hiram in *early admission*, and no offense but he's kind of a jerk. That combined score of 1600 on the SATs doesn't tell the whole story. Example: He asked my friend Kelly to the homecoming dance and then *withdrew the invitation* when she cut her hair short, saying, and I quote, that he "wasn't into girls with short hair." Not only *that*, but he went on to ask *another* girl, who also had short hair, which makes him a complete and total LIAR! So I mean. Let me in.

You might be wondering why I'd want to go to the same school as Dennis Hiram, but I wanted to go way before Dennis even *applied*. In *fact*, I'm the one who gave him the idea to apply. Because he was all like, "I don't care where I go, where should I go?" (I mean, seriously, he's about as deep as an ice tray.)

Is it my fault that you're one of the "hot schools" and super-selective now? Is it my fault that all the baby boomers decided to spawn at exactly the same time? Is it my fault there's like this digitally mastered army of college applicants? I've wanted to go there *forever*, ever since I visited my sister's friend Helen and there was this party in the New Apartments where I hooked up with this . . . I mean, it just affirmed my desire to attend a small liberal arts college, with a strong faculty and a tight-knit community.

I admit that I was a *little* disappointed to discover there's no skiing nearby, and that the nearest city is like seven hours away, unless you count Columbus, which I don't, or Cleveland, which I double-don't. And *ideally*, the drama department would do more musicals and I wouldn't have to take the old-book courses in the English department, but whatever.

Between you and me, once I get that letter—which by now I hope you've decided to send me since my life will totally suck if you don't—I'm going to quit *everything* and sleep late, read nothing but the J. Crew catalog, go to the tanning bed, and *veg* . . . I mean, just to mentally *prepare* myself to start classes at a small liberal arts school, with a strong faculty and a tight-knit community.

And a single would be nice.

Part 2

. . . .

From the Outsiders

How to Get into College Without Really Trying

. . . .

Gail Hudson

September

WHEN MY DAUGHTER was younger, I hated it when parents would say to me in an ominous tone, "Just wait until she becomes a teenager." But today I heard myself using that exact same voice with an innocent mother of a middle schooler. "Just wait until she starts applying to college."

The general rule of advice for parents of high school seniors is this: Let the students run this show; give them the responsibility to make it happen. Our role as parents is simply to be their support staff.

As far as I can tell, my daughter's version of "running the show" means avoiding all discussion of college applications. "I'm too tired to talk about it now," she tells me on her way upstairs for a shower. Or, "I'm too busy, can we do this later?" as she heads into a corner of the house to practice piano. The problem is she is tired, or busy, all of the time.

· · · · · · ·

SENIORS DON'T WANT their parents taking over the application process. At least that's what the college advisor I hired tells me when I called her today. That's right, I hired a college advisor. My daughter goes to a public high school of sixteen hundred students, with four hundred students per guidance counselor. For one hundred dollars an hour, I hired someone to do what my child won't let me do and the high school guidance counselor doesn't have time to do—go over all of my daughter's academic and social interests, research the schools that match those interests, then make a reasonable list of choices.

I also thought a college advisor would give her a little bit of an edge. The first time we met with the college advisor, in fact, was just after my daughter finished her sophomore year.

"This is a little early," she told me. "Most parents start talking with me toward the end of the junior year."

I felt embarrassed by my display of anxiety, but also relieved that Gabrielle was a step ahead of the others.

Everyone wants to know where she is applying to college. In certain circles, this list contains an unspoken code: super-high achiever (Ivy League), medium-high achiever (small, private liberal arts), all the way down to slacker (local community college).

I realize this is elitist and superficial, but sometimes I find myself rising to the competitive bait. There I am in the neighborhood video store or the grocery checkout line, name-dropping the schools Gabrielle's considering, all the places we've visited, and hungrily listening to the other students' lists. I hate this about myself, but I can't seem to stop. It's the playground scene all over again: whose kid is walking, whose kid can climb the ladder alone. When will it ever end?

· · · · · · ·

THE COLLEGE ADVISOR insists that I stop making the appointments for my daughter—she can use the phone, she can e-mail, she knows where to find me. You need to let her own this, she tells me. If she can't step into it, maybe she's just not ready to go to college.

I try taking a casual approach. "So how's it going with the college stuff?"

"It's not working," Gabrielle tells me. "Your anxiety is oozing out of every pore in your body. It's contaminating the room."

If I stop holding the anxiety, she will have to hold it. I know this. And, yet, holding anxiety is like holding on to control.

It's hard to let go and trust that it's all going to be okay.

October

I GET A letter from the high school. My daughter has four unexcused absences from her AP art class. Two more absences and she is in danger of getting a grade of NC, the letter states—No Credit. I immediately grab the calculator and tally how this will affect her GPA. Okay, studio art is not a core curriculum grade, but it is what she wants to major in at college. An NC would reduce her GPA an entire one-tenth of a point. Gabrielle's a National Latin Scholar, her SATs are stellar, but her GPA has been mysteriously slipping lately.

I confront her when she returns from school.

"Come on," she says. "I can't believe you think I would actually fail art." Her face is smudged with charcoal, and she has crusted acrylic paint under her fingernails. "It's just that art is my first class after lunch, and if I'm more than five minutes late, she has to mark it as an absence. You can call her. I never miss a class."

This soothes me. But in the middle of the night, I wake up fuming. Why does she have to be late after lunch? If she screws up this art grade, I will scream my head off at her. I'll make her pay for this.

I make some warm milk. My anger feels all confused.

· · · · · · · ·

BEING A PARENT of a high school senior is like a spiritual practice. Don't attach to the fear. Don't attach to future outcomes. Just be in the now. Sometimes, I can be a little Buddha—knowing that it doesn't really matter where she goes to college. She has straight teeth. She knows how to ride a horse and fast-pitch a softball. She is smart, funny, and creative. She has parents, grandparents, uncles, aunts, cousins, neighbors, family friends who would do anything for her. These are the assets that will help her most in life. Sure, there is statistical evidence that you can get higher-paying jobs with a degree from MIT versus the local community college. But more income doesn't necessarily mean more happiness. Education can't buy us loving spouses and joyful lives. How can I know all this and still be so anxious?

· · · · · · ·

IT IS LATE on Sunday night, and Gabrielle is overwhelmed. She asks me to sit on her bed with her. All weekend, she gave herself to everyone else's demands: a friend with a personal crisis, a boyfriend who wanted to go out, a family that needed a last-minute babysitter. Now she is angry, tearful, anxious, behind at school before the week has even started. "And this whole college application thing is feeling like way too much pressure." I want to fix it for her, give her advice on how to make it all better. But instead I ask questions. How can you stay in touch with your own needs? How can you make yourself the priority?

An hour later, I go to bed worried that we'll never find the right college for her. I don't want her to enter into a pressure cooker. But I do want her to get into a school that will help her stretch and grow.

I fall asleep wondering, *Will we ever find a place that will hold her and love her as well as I do?*

November

I AM A WRITER by profession and make a living editing and teaching others to write. Do you think my daughter would let me have just one quick look at her personal essay? No.

We strike a deal. Here is what I cannot do to help: I cannot look at her essay, or look at her applications, or look up deadlines for when her applications are due, or ask her any questions about how it is going.

Here is what I can do to help: address envelopes.

One stack goes to the high school for sending out her transcripts. One stack goes to the teachers she's asking for recommendations. I ask her where the envelopes are that she'll use for the applications. "No one does it that way anymore," she says. "It's all done online these days."

· · · · · · · ·

TONIGHT GABRIELLE GOES online to submit her application to UCLA. It's due December 1, tomorrow. But apparently, every student has waited until Thanksgiving weekend to work on his or her application and is now trying to send it through the Internet on Sunday night. The system is jammed, and she can't send the application she has worked so hard on. "Oh, well. I didn't care that much about UCLA anyway," she says, switching off the computer and heading upstairs to bed.

Her first application deadline. Come and missed. I am left standing in the kitchen, jaw slack, dish towel dangling limp at my side.

December

GABRIELLE COMES TO me and says, "I want to be an artist—a real artist, not a commercial artist. That's my gift, I'm sure of it." Her hair is in French braids. She is wearing her high school sweatshirt and sipping chamomile tea. She tells me she can't imagine a life where she isn't doing art every day. Then she asks if I have ever heard of a school that lets the students decide what they want to learn about and provides the resources to go as deep and as long as the student wants.

The only school I know of that lets students do this is her preschool.

Maybe college isn't even the right track for her. We just assume that the smart, enthusiastic, and, yes, privileged high school seniors will head straight to college. But my daughter seems more drawn to "life education" these days. She tells me that she learned more confidence and useful skills at the wilderness horseback riding camp where she works in the summer than she has from all her high school classes this year.

. . . .

SHE HAS DECIDED that her senior art project will be on homeless people.

January

AS SHE IS going out the door to school, my daughter tells me that she had a dream about skating on thin ice. In the dream, a girl fell through the cracks in front of her and pulled down my daughter's coat and cell phone with her. My daughter couldn't save her.

"Hey, by the way, have you seen that application to NYU?" she asks, a cell phone in one hand, a travel mug of hot chai tea in the other hand, and a piece of buttered toast dangling from her mouth. "Oh, never mind," she says through the toast, pulling the application out of her messenger bag.

"Don't get chai or toast butter on it," I shout after her. She rolls her eyes and pulls the door closed behind her with her foot.

. . . .

I KNOW THE January 15 deadlines are coming up—but I am keeping with my agreement and not mentioning it.

· · · · · · ·

IT'S 9:30 P.M. on January 14, and my daughter comes to me as I'm closing out the kitchen for the night. "I need your help," she says. "Will you look at my essay?"

Here's the trap. At this hour, a rewrite is out of the question. A revision isn't even possible. What could possibly come of my looking at her essay the night before it has to be sent? I could lovingly offer her a wonderful life lesson about taking responsibility for her own procrastination and simply say, "I'm sorry, but I'm too tired." And then go off to bed, leaving her standing slack-jawed in the kitchen. Or I could read her essay, hope it's fine, and if it isn't, push up my sleeves and spend the next three hours helping her make it right. Is this a situation where I can let her fail? Or do I rescue her?

I look at her closely. She has a smattering of stress pimples on her forehead. "Please," she asks, her post-braces retainer making her lisp so that it comes out "Pleathe." I push up my sleeves and follow her to the computer.

· · · · · · ·

ESSAY DONE. I helped her with it only a little. Okay, more than a little. It took about three hours, but it's a winner. I hope we get in.

· · · · · · ·

IT IS NOW 5:40 P.M. on the evening of January 15, and I am relieved and thrilled that the first round of applications are done, presumably sent into cyberspace hours ago. All we have left are two applications to art colleges, not due until mid-February.

I am making one of Gabrielle's favorite dinners—a curry dish from *The Vegetarian Epicure*—just to celebrate this great accomplishment. One-half teaspoon cumin. One teaspoon turmeric. One-half teaspoon cayenne. My daughter enters the room.

"I need some help finishing my applications."

"What? You're not done?" I accidentally drop a whole table-spoon of cayenne into the pot. I scrape the red clump of cayenne out of the orange mush of spices. "Why didn't you send it online?"

Gabrielle informs me that she sent her general applications online, but one school wants a graded essay that has to be mailed separately. Something my daughter failed to check until this morning. She doesn't seem aware that this is my "I told you so" moment. I continue to stir.

"Here are my options," she continues. "A short essay about *The Canterbury Tales* or a five-page essay about *Beowulf*."

I look at the clock. It's 5:45. I'm pretty sure the post office closes at 6:00. It has to be postmarked today. "Let me see them," I suggest, reaching for my reading glasses. I give them both a cursory scan. "Go with the Beowulf," I say.

"Could you at least read them?" she pleads.

I have a string of measuring spoons in my fist, and my fingers are stained with spices. The buttery curry paste in the pot needs stirring or it's going to burn. "Read them? Now?" I ask. I want to shout, "THIS IS IT! THERE IS NO MORE FRICKIN TIME."

I tersely explain the post office issue. "You can't just drop it in the nearest mailbox and have it postmarked for today." Believe me, I've been there. I know all about manuscripts that have to be postmarked that day. I've ridden this edge, before faxes and e-mails. "You have to choose an essay now. Use your own judgment. Then get in the car and drive to the post office."

"All right, it's *Beowulf*," she says, folding it into the envelope. "But can you drive me to the nearest post office? I don't know how to get there."

How will this girl ever survive on her own? I turn off the stove.

Driving downtown toward the post office, I do what any self-respecting parent would do in this moment. I shame her. "This is really annoying. You should have taken care of all this earlier."

She swivels her entire body toward me, voice escalating. "When exactly would I have time to do this today? I was at school until four, and then I had a piano lesson."

"I mean earlier, as in two months ago."

She looks out the window. It's 5:55 P.M. And dark and raining.

We pull into the post office at 5:58. The sign says it closes at 6:30. We're half an hour early.

"See. We had plenty of time," she tells me, huffing out of the car.

. . . .

GABRIELLE INVITES ME to look at one of the art school catalogs with her tonight. As we're flipping through the pages, she suddenly gets teary. "I can't do this," she says. "I don't want to leave my friends, or my school, or even my family. This whole college pressure is horrible. I hate how it forces you to leave the life you love."

· · · · · · ·

WE ASK GABRIELLE to pick up her clutter around the house before she heads out tonight. "I am so ready to move out of here," she mutters, gathering up her five coats, four purses, and nine pairs of shoes.

February

GABRIELLE HAS WORKED all month on getting her art materials sent out to the two art schools she is applying to. The dining room table has been turned into her studio—chalk, acrylics, charcoal sketches splayed everywhere. I have been impressed with her diligence. It feels like she has figured out what she cares about and has been willing to commit herself to it.

Now it is the day that all her materials must be sent by overnight mail. "Mama," she calls out as I walk past the dining room. "Could you please help me with my application?"

"I thought this was all you had to do. There's an application, too?" Body getting hot. Heart pumping.

"I know. It's just way too much," she says, as if we're complaining about the art school's demands and not her complete disorganization. "But it's only a formality—they mostly care about the art. Anyway, I'm a little behind, and I was wondering if you could just type in the answers to some of the questions that I haven't finished yet while I finish this watercolor." She swishes her brush in a glass of murky water.

I pull up the "routine" application on the computer, expecting a name, address, and extracurricular activities kind of application. I discover questions such as, "Do you think it's important that artists speak or write about their work?" and "Describe an event or idea that has been very important to you." Most of them are answered, as she promised, but there are a few that are blank.

As I start to scroll through the application, there's a knock at the door. The cable guy is here. I forgot. Today is the day I scheduled to have my Internet cable installed. It took me weeks to get this appointment. I lead him into my office. "Can you turn off the computer for a while?" he asks, holding up a drill.

It is after 3:00. The entire package has to be at the UPS Store by 4:00. "No," I say. "We're working on a college application."

"We?" he asks, raising an eyebrow.

I resist the urge to explain myself, explain the whole mess of procrastination and ambivalence that's plagued our house since September. "Yep. Down to the wire here. So can I keep it on while you work?" I turn my face to the screen and call out to my daughter. "Okay, we're going to have to talk over the drilling."

Somehow we get it done. My daughter and I grab her artwork. I print out her application, and we jump in the car. As I speed toward the UPS Store, she sprays hairspray on all her chalk drawings. We arrive with nine minutes to spare.

. . . .

ON THE WAY home, I turn to her at a stoplight and lay my hand atop hers. "Why has this been so hard to do ahead of time?" I ask.

Gabrielle is silent for a moment. "Maybe the reason I waited so long is that I'm afraid I won't get in anywhere." The Seattle winter sun is low in the sky, giving her face a golden-pink sheen. "Maybe it would feel really horrible to try my very hardest and be rejected. If I slap it all together at the last minute and I don't get in anywhere, at least I could tell myself that I didn't really try that hard."

March

THIS IS THE waiting month. There is nothing I can say or do to help, but I try anyway.

"The truth is, I really believe you will get accepted somewhere," I tell Gabrielle as she eats Heath Bar Crunch ice cream straight from the carton. "But if you don't, we'll just start looking into other options. I know you'll find your way."

She smiles weakly and continues scooping. Six rejections—could one high school girl hold that much disappointment?

April

THE SIX RESULTS are in. Two rejections—one from her "safety" and one from her "reach" school. Two wait lists—both from schools she liked. Two acceptances—one from the school she liked the least and one from the art school that she most wanted to get into. It's a good list—some disappointments, but much elation, too. We open a bottle of champagne, toast her, and call the grandparents.

"She got into her first-choice school," I tell my mother on the phone, watching Gabrielle twirl around the kitchen with her father. I mentally note that I have used the word "she" instead of "we." The cable guy was right. Hard as I've tried this year, I haven't been successful at extracting myself from the process.

Maybe now, I can finally let go.

May

TONIGHT, GABRIELLE PRESENTS her senior art project at the high school. As it turns out, she did indeed make portraits of homeless people, some of whom she met while handing out sandwiches to men and women living on the streets. But she also made portraits of people from other walks of life—strangers on city buses, her close friends, her younger brother, even us, her parents. She tells the audience that each portrait, like each person, had a life of its own. As a creator, it was sometimes challenging to let the art be what it wanted to be.

I think back to when she was in preschool so many years ago—the one that let her go as long and as deep as she yearned to. Gabrielle spent her time drawing portraits of unicorn ponies surrounded by swirly purple flowers and fat yellow suns. Her resources were as follows: a box of markers, an endless supply of scrap paper, and permission to do what she loved.

Seeing her now, with her collection of painted canvases, I realize it doesn't really matter where she goes to college. Yes, this Buddha moment is partially sponsored by the fact that she got into a school of her choice. But for tonight, I know with certainty that she is on a path that will take her as far and as deep as she wants to go. As for the resources? Just look at her. She already possesses everything she needs to find her way.

Postscript

OVER THE SUMMER, Gabrielle decides to defer college for a year. She's clear that it's the right choice for a number of reasons: the obvious ambivalence she's felt all along, her desire to travel and get a non-classroom education for a while. Her school has allowed her to postpone her enrollment to the following fall. She has saved up enough money to travel through the South Pacific with a friend for six months.

It is now late November, one week before her departure. Gabrielle comes to me, a mug of green tea between the palms of her hands, as if in prayer.

"I've been thinking. I'm not sure that art school is going to be enough for me. I also want to learn more about international politics. So I'd like to apply to a few more schools before I leave. Do you think I have time to pull together a new essay before I go?"

The Age of Reasons

·······

Joe Queenan

Shortly after entering his sophomore year in high school, my sixteen-year-old son began talking about attending college in Philadelphia. This warmed the cockles of my heart, as I am a native of the City of Brotherly Love and a graduate of St. Joseph's, a venerable Jesuit university. Moreover, because Philadelphia is only 130 miles from my home in Tarrytown, New York, Gordon's enrollment would allow me to keep my eye on him. Frankly, I never trusted the kid.

But when I asked Gordon precisely where he was thinking of applying, his response was vague. He didn't want to go to the same university I had gone to. He knew I would not pay for him to attend Villanova, because the Wildcats are the hated crosstown rivals of St. Joe's Hawks. He didn't seem to know much about Penn or Temple, had never heard of La Salle, wouldn't have been able to pick Drexel University out of a police lineup. So why, exactly, did he want to go to school in the city of my birth?

"I love the Eagles," he said, referring to Philadelphia's beloved but underachieving professional football team.

"I love the Eagles, too," I replied, even-temperedly. "But you can't go to college in Philadelphia just because you love a football team that happens to play there. Any guidance counselor can tell you that."

"Why not?" he demanded.

"Because the college-selection process has to be rigorous, meticulous, and nuanced," I informed him. "Because where you go to college will affect your prospects for employment, your lifetime income, and ultimately your happiness. You can't decide where to go to college simply because you like the city's football team."

He considered my rebuttal. Then he spoke.

"Well, I also like the 76ers."

"I can see you've given this a lot of thought."

Voluminous, though entirely unscientific, research into this subject apprises me that conversations of this nature are by no means uncommon. One close friend told me her son had chosen a nondescript college in the rural hinterland because "it's a party school, and it's close to another party school—also, he could get in." Another chose a college in Colorado because he loves to ski. A third opted for the Midwest so she could be far away from her parents, and a fourth selected a university in Upstate New York so she could be close to her boyfriend. Now that she has broken up with her boyfriend, it is not clear that she is happy with her choice.

Much as parents would like to think that their children attack the college selection process with the same neurotic zeal that they do, this is generally not the case. When my daughter was applying two years ago, it was clear that rock 'n' roll played an enormous role in determining her choices. No matter how prestigious certain groves of academe might purport to be, if they were not in a booming metropolis with lots of clubs hold-ing cheap concerts, she was not applying.

Though legitimate factors like freezing temperatures in Ithaca, urban squalor in New Haven, and elitist dining clubs in Princeton entered into her reasoning, it was always clear that the influence of Weezer, Matchbox Twenty, and The Strokes far outweighed the influence of Albert Einstein, Saul Bellow, and Milton Friedman. So Boston got the nod.

Experts in this area always warn high school seniors to re-sist the wheedling, cajoling, and outright threats of their par-ents and to choose a college based on their own needs. For parents, this is a bitter pill to swallow. From the moment I swaddled my son in his first leprechaun layette set, I nour-ished the hope that he would fulfill my generic Irish Catholic dreams and attend Notre Dame. Those dreams have now been shattered.

"I'm not going to school in Indiana," my son informed me when I raised the subject last year. At the time, the Fighting Irish football team was 8-0 and number one in the *New York Times* computer rankings. Notre Dame was also a very good school.

"If you can go to school in Philadelphia just because you like the Eagles," I parried, "why can't you go to school in South Bend, Indiana, just because you like the Fighting Irish?"

"Because I've been to Indiana, Dad," he fired back. Dam-nation. Whatever had possessed me to take him on that sum-mer jaunt across the nation's heartland two years ago? Why couldn't I have taken the safe route and shielded his eyes from the eerie blandness of Indianapolis, the bland eeriness of Fort

Wayne, and the abject horror of Gary, which would have given its municipal eyeteeth to be either bland or eerie.

A born hustler, still clinging to those fading dreams of glorious afternoons cheek by jowl with my son in the shadow of Touchdown Jesus, I quickly regrouped.

"Notre Dame has nothing to do with the rest of Indiana," I argued. "It's a pristine island that lies outside the Hoosier archipelago. Besides," I chided him, "going to Notre Dame isn't just about football. Notre Dame is the mystical cradle of the Irish-American dream, the repository of our Celtic hopes, the spawning ground of our Hibernian reveries, the incubator of our most fiercely beloved stereotypes."

"It's in Indiana, Dad. Forget it."

As I reflected on my son's intransigence, I glumly realized that the crabapple fell not far from the tree. Though I like to think that I went to St. Joe's because it was all the way over on the other side of Philadelphia from my home on West Oak Lane, and therefore somewhat exotic, the real reason I went was because it had a fantastic basketball team. Naturally conservative, if not reactionary, I was also impressed that St. Joe's required students to take eighteen credits of theology and philosophy, and maintained a strict dress code: maroon blazer, white shirt, gray trousers, maroon tie. Never mind that the year I entered the dress code was dropped and I instantaneously morphed into a sock-scorning, hirsute, atheistic hippie. It was the principle of the thing.

Still, I didn't go to St. Joe's because I liked the maroon blazers or the teachings of St. Thomas Aquinas. It was definitely a basketball thing.

In the end, I have come to accept that if it was okay for me to choose a college because it had an outstanding basketball team (though tiny, it has produced a fistful of highly regarded NBA coaches, including Jack Ramsay, Jack McKinney, and Jimmy Lynam), it is okay for my son to choose a college because it happens to be in the same city as the Philadelphia Eagles. Now all he has to do is decide where he wants to go, and get a 1550 on the SATs so he can corral some scholarship money to help Dad. Penn would be great. Haverford would be wonderful. St. Joe's or La Salle would be fantastic. Drexel would be splendid. Temple would pass muster. Even Philadelphia University would do.

But if he applies to Villanova, I'm disowning him.

Application Madness

....

Anne C. Roark

I knew we were in trouble when I started rearranging the furniture in our family room.

At first, the changes were inconsequential—a couch pushed aside, a library table installed in front of the television. But then things grew more complicated. I dragged in a round table from the garden, and chairs from the kitchen, and scavenged a bunker-sized bulletin board from my office. We needed a place to post deadlines, keep track of names, and record other intelligence gathered.

The mail had already begun to pile up, sending me on a frantic search for storage files. I improvised with a set of large wooden crates, which my friend Gracie had left in my care after her fiancé found out they were a gift from one of her old boyfriends.

Then came the most drastic step of all: I began emptying bookshelves (fiction stayed, but philosophy and poetry were wiped out altogether) to make room for our new collection of six- and seven-hundred-page guidebooks. They were mostly filled with propaganda, but some offered strategy options and collected data that might be useful, and even practice drills.

All this may sound like someone on a compulsive reorganization rampage. But I was dealing with a much more serious problem: Our firstborn child, Kate, now a senior in high school, was preparing to apply to college. Our family room was about to become Command Central for an uncertain campaign that lay ahead.

My husband Marshall and I had always assumed our children would go to college, but we had no particular place in mind. He graduated from a college everyone in the world knew about, while I went to a college almost no one had even heard of. Yet we both ended up in pretty much the same place: living in a crazy city, making less money than we wanted (but more than we needed), doing work we loved to hate and hated to love, and raising children we idolized but who felt about us much the way we felt about our careers (loved to hate, etc.). Out of that experience, we became what you might call college admissions pacifists.

• • • • • • •

I SWORE NEVER to be one of those hysterical parents who are convinced their children's fates—their careers and lives—are determined by where they go to college. My children's acceptance (or rejection) by a particular institution would not be the ultimate test of my mettle as a parent. I was especially offended by the feverish slogans tossed about by so many parents: Berkeley or Bust, Princeton or Perish, Harvard or Hang (Yourself). These struck me as the worst kind of academic xenophobia.

A few years earlier, poolside during a family vacation in Hawaii, my resolve had been momentarily tested. I was cornered by a talkative father who bragged about how he was gaming the college admissions system on his daughter's behalf. He had been driven to it, he said, by the frightful competition to enroll. I expressed surprise: "It seems to me that it's easier to get into college today than it has ever been."

That set him off. "Let me tell you," he said. "These places are so swamped with applications that they can now afford to wait-list students with 1500 SATs and A-minus averages."

Worried that his daughter would be shut out, he had sought the advice of a consultant who specialized in college admissions.

"This woman," he said, "takes one look at our daughter's application—which is pretty impressive, I've got to tell you—and she is ready to toss it in the trash. 'They see a million of these,' she tells me. 'Good grades, good test scores, good athlete, good recommendations, good prep school. We've got to do something to make her stand out.'

"So here's what this woman does," he went on. "She creates a new profile for our daughter—a whole new persona. No more talk about loving math and science and wanting to be a doctor. She doesn't care if the kid's already a doctor. Brown and Yale are overloaded with them already. She notices our daughter has taken some Latin, so she tells her to downplay the math and science, and announce her intention of majoring in classics. That should impress them!"

Evidently, it didn't. Marshall and I found out much later that the big guns turned the daughter down. So did most of the medium-sized guns. We didn't hear it from the father, but friends of friends told us that the girl was fine with the outcome and eventually loved where she ended up. The father was said to be still recovering.

· · · · · · ·

I FOUND HIS story vaguely amusing and a little tawdry, but also troubling. If the competition had become that fierce, perhaps my husband and I should reexamine our serene attitude about which college to attend and how to get in. Sure, neither of our two daughters was in high school yet, but maybe it was time to do something.

When I broached the subject with Marshall, he became enraged. The only way I could calm him down was to promise never to reinvent our children as classics majors, not even if they begged us.

· · · · · · ·

ONCE THE FAMILY room was reasonably well organized, I settled down with our stack of college guides. There were insider's guides and outsider's guides, compilations of the best colleges and compendiums of even better colleges; testimonials on colleges that made a difference in lives and exposés of colleges that had no impact.

The more I read them, the more I began to think our boorish friend in Hawaii hadn't been as alarmist as he seemed. Colleges I'd never heard of, some more obscure than my own alma mater, were turning down 40, 50, 60 percent of their applicants. Competition at the brand-name schools had gone beyond the ridiculous.

Then I recalled hearing an administrator at Harvard trying to explain to a group of alumni why the university was turning away so many of their brilliant little legacies. In one year alone, he said, the undergraduate admissions office rejects enough valedictorians to fill the freshman class four times over. Or was it the entire undergraduate college? I couldn't remember, although with that kind of competition, I wasn't sure it made any difference.

Stanford administrators were telling their alumni virtually the same thing. Not only were they turning away students who had been first in their classes, they were turning away valedictorians who had perfect 1600 scores on their SATs. There just wasn't room for all of them. I began to feel uneasy. I should have had a better fix on the situation. After all, I had written extensively about colleges and universities as a journalist in Washington and Los Angeles some years earlier, and had even done a stint as a college admissions officer. Clearly, I had been away from it too long. I needed to know more.

That is how I found myself packing to attend the annual meeting of the National Association for College Admission Counseling in Long Beach, California. I had covered the organization from time to time in the mid-1970s. Maybe, I thought, I can get some inside tips, or a least some perspective.

"You're not going to talk to any of the colleges I'm interested in, are you?" my daughter asked with alarm.

"No, this is purely professional," I said, trying to be the cool, inquisitive reporter rather than the frantic mother.

"I'm just going to poke around and see if there are any trends worth writing about.

"There are some sessions about problem parents that look interesting," I told my husband. "If I pick up any tips, I'll let you know."

"You'll fit right in," he assured me.

. . . .

THE LONG BEACH Convention Center is a large, glassy structure overlooking the city's harbor. Despite the warm and sunny
Southern California day, people were milling about in tweed
jackets and sweater vests, looking very East Coast. I didn't
know when I had seen so many men in bow ties—or, for that
matter, any kind of ties. It was similarly odd to see so many
women walking around with fully covered midriffs.

I went in search of someone who could answer my questions, and managed to snag the director of college counseling
at a high-powered New York prep school. "There's been a sea
change," he said as we sat outside on some steps. When he
started in the business in 1985, he talked to students about
"good choices, colleges that matched their interests, were the
right size, in the right location. Now it's all about strategy.
They want to know, 'What's the best place I can get in, and
how do I go about doing it?'"

There are plenty of colleges and universities in the country,
he said, about two thousand in all. The problem is with the
seventy-five that are really competitive, he said, referring to
those colleges where fewer than half of the applicants are admitted. More eighteen-year-olds are applying to those seventy-
five colleges today than ever before. Moreover, there is a higher
percentage of *smart* eighteen-year-olds in the applicant pool.

"Let me give you the history behind this," my New York
expert said. In the 1960s, as the postwar baby boom generation crowded into the system, colleges and universities built
new facilities and enlarged their faculties. By the mid-1970s,
the boom had collapsed, brought down by a deepening popu-

lation trough. Private colleges and universities struggled to attract students. Top colleges hired publicists and mounted recruiting and advertising campaigns. Prestigious universities in the Northeast began reaching into public schools in the South and Midwest and plucking out the best graduates. Soon, the smartest student in a high school in Arizona no longer settled for an honors program in a state university. That same kid was now applying to Yale.

Colleges and universities that had long had excellent reputations in their own regions but were largely unknown elsewhere also began national recruiting campaigns. Institutions no one had heard of one year became hot tickets the next; their applications doubled and tripled. Small colleges and medium-sized universities that had once been open to strong students suddenly found themselves wait-listing super ones.

That was when students began to panic. Seeing colleges turn down fully qualified applicants for no apparent reason except that there were too many fully qualified applicants, students began to see the admissions process as a game of luck. To increase their odds of winning, students started doubling or tripling the number of applications they submitted. This made college admissions committees crazy because the more applications they got, the less sure they were about whom to admit.

"Which brings us," the New York counselor said, "to where we are today, which is that everyone, almost, is pretty much consistently hysterical."

No one more so than parents. In fact, the conference program listed three panel discussions on how to deal with anxious parents. I picked "Parents: the Good, the Bad, and the Hysterical." By the time I got there, they had evidently finished with the "good" part and were jumping back and forth between "bad" and "hysterical." One admissions director recounted a conversation he had had with an applicant. When asked how many colleges he was applying to, the student replied, "I'm applying to three colleges; my dad's applying to six."

Next there was a recounting of e-mails from parents to directors of admissions: One mother expressed anxiety about what her daughter would eat; another sent in her laundry list of questions about the laundry service; a third mother wanted a rating of the air quality in dormitories; a fourth inquired about the availability of a single room for her son who had suffered a football injury.

A high school counselor, standing to ask a question of the panel, sheepishly admitted to being a mother herself. I began to wonder why only mothers were being singled out. Was there some parental gender stereotyping going on here? Were female parents more obnoxious than their male counterparts? While I was cogitating on this, another high school college counselor stood up and told a father story. A particularly pesky father had been stalking her with college admissions questions. He managed to track her down in a hospital an hour after she was wheeled out of a delivery room. "He wanted to talk about his daughter's SAT scores."

The audience guffawed, but I got up and left. I wasn't embarrassed or offended so much as worried. There I was in Long Beach, doing nothing. I hadn't sent e-mails to admissions directors or stalked a single high school counselor. I didn't even know the name of my daughter's counselor. I had allowed myself to think that helping my daughter apply to college was going to be a smooth and quick operation. In fact, it was beginning to seem a bit like the war in Iraq: a protracted mission with no clear plan.

· · · · · · ·

BACK IN THE family room, daughter Kate was online investigating colleges. She was very clear about her academic priorities: a great international relations program (she loved history and had become a political junkie) and an even better studio arts program (she was an accomplished artist). Having spent two and a half years in a huge public, highly diverse, urban high school in Los Angeles, she wanted to chuck large and public but was determined to hang on to urban and diverse. She liked the idea of old buildings nestled in beautiful surroundings, walking distance from swank shops, magnificent museums, renowned restaurants. The emerging profile was that of a small, private liberal arts college located in a city, preferably on the East Coast. Middlebury in Manhattan, maybe? Williams in Washington? While Kate took virtual tours of classrooms and dormitories, I was doing my best to remain calm, having just discovered that she didn't know her college counselor either. She was a senior and an honors student taking a slew of Advanced Placement classes, which would suggest she was eligible for college counseling. But two counselors in a school with 3,800 students didn't have time to do much counseling. They had sent home with each senior a package of college application materials and instructions on

how to fill them out. One assignment was to write a recommendation about yourself "from the point of view of your
counselor." This did not bode well.

. . . .

"YOU NEED A professional," my husband's friend David told
me. He had a friend who had talked her way into an Ivy
League college and, realizing she had a marketable talent, had
since become a private admissions counselor. Now she helped
other determined applicants talk, test, write, play, paint—
whatever it took—their way into the college of their dreams.

I was mildly skeptical. I had been told the first thing a college counselor tells parents is to stop saying "we" when talking about your child's college applications. "These are not our
applications; they are hers. We are not applying to college; she
is." Right. Just like she's paying the $40,000 it costs to attend
a private college for one year, or—if we were to be so lucky—
the $10,000 to $15,000 it would cost to stay in state.

Setting aside my doubts, I called David's friend in New
York. Her receptionist said the woman was too swamped to
get on the phone and say hello—business was that good. But
not to worry. They would send me to their new Los Angeles
office where I could customize a program for Kate. And the
cost? Not to worry.

I don't know why I wasn't more surprised when the list arrived and I saw the prices. I just assumed $28,000 was a typo-
graphical error. When I called the receptionist back, she said
not to worry; we didn't need all the services in the $28,000
package. We could probably get by with something more
modest, say, in the $17,000 or $18,000 range.

I told her I thought $1,700 was too much, that $170 was closer to what I was thinking. This time she didn't tell me not to worry. "You get what you pay for," she said.

· · · · · · ·

I TRIED AGAIN with a college counselor who made house calls for $170 an hour. Her first suggestion was a college on board a ship. We reminded her of my daughter's desires—a small liberal arts college near a city on the East Coast. The woman moved on land, but she wasn't any more helpful. She came up with a list of seventy-five or so colleges that would be "perfect" for Kate, forgot to leave it with us, and that was the end of her.

We were on our own again. Kate was interviewing with college representatives who were visiting her school from all over the country. Marshall and I were organizing trips with our daughter to prospective campuses in the East and Midwest. Who needs experts?

· · · · · · ·

BY NOW, I was well versed in the admissions strategy most often touted by private counselors. It was a simple formula:

First, pick three target schools. Those are the ones that should accept your child because her grades and test scores match those of the students who are already there. (The operative word is "should." Remember, there are no guarantees in this business.)

Next, pick three "reach" schools, where your child's test scores and grades look competitive but really aren't because there are so many applicants with similar qualifications.

Usually reach schools aren't any better than target schools but for some reason have more cachet.

(Caution: Don't confuse reach schools with beyond-reach schools. Most beyond-reach schools come with full bragging rights, which makes them difficult to evaluate, but not necessarily the right choice even if your child got in, which odds are she won't.)

Next, settle on three safety schools. These are colleges that will probably accept your child whether she wants to be accepted or not. Unless, of course, they, too, are suddenly deluged with applications.

If that should happen, go immediately to Plan LD. Late decision is essentially a behind-the-scenes triage system that matches overlooked students with one of the country's 1,925 schools that still have room even after the admissions process has officially ended. The good news is that some of them are sleepers, good colleges that have yet to be discovered. Until that happens, they will probably be happy to take a look at an overlooked student or two.

· · · · · · ·

"THAT'S NOT THE way to do it!" Henry said, pounding his fist on the table. Henry, a friend for over twenty years, normally was not a fist pounder. But his daughter was also applying to college and he was showing the strain.

He had just finished reading a study published by Harvard University that provided incontrovertible evidence that applying via early decision significantly improved an applicant's chances of being admitted to a highly selective college. It was the equivalent of boosting SAT scores by one hundred points.

It could double—sometimes triple—the odds favoring admission to a prestigious college or university. The study, published in a book entitled *The Early Decision Game*, was based on analysis of 500,000 applications at fourteen schools. I'd heard some of this before, but assumed it was just one of the many theories parents pass around without any evidence to support it. Henry, however, was a statistics stud (he knew, for example, the career batting average of every important Los Angeles Dodger for the last forty years, and remembered the SAT scores of all of his college roommates). When it came to college admissions data, I figured if Henry said it was true, it had to be true. My husband, a statistics fanatic himself who regularly sparred with Henry over sports trivia, was skeptical. Our daughter, he pointed out, had so much going for her. She had done her SAT prep classes and brought her scores up three hundred points. She had As in her AP classes and was passing all her AP exams with flying colors. She'd spent the summer at the Rhode Island School of Design, painting. The summer before, she'd been in Paris, drawing. She was bright and talented—this was her father talking—and shouldn't be asked to limit herself to one school as required by early decision. She should play the field for as long as possible.

It was true that she was in love with a dozen schools, all different from one another: Barnard, Bowdoin, Brown, Colby, Connecticut College, Carnegie Mellon, the University of Chicago, the University of Pennsylvania, Haverford, Vassar, Wesleyan, Washington University in St. Louis—to name a few. But I knew the blush would wear off and she'd start dumping the ones that had baggage she couldn't handle. She could deal with St. Louis, Providence, even Pittsburgh. But Poughkeepsie?

No way. Bowdoin was too cold; Barnard was cold in a different way. The tour guide at Wesleyan had an attitude.

Let's face it, there are problems with all of them. Why not have her pick one now and get it over with?

But most schools use a common application form, so why shouldn't she give them all a chance?

Because she'll have less of a chance.

But what if she goes for early decision and doesn't get in? She'll be devastated.

She'll be more devastated if she gets twelve rejections.

Why do you always have to worry so much? She's going to get in everywhere she applies.

Kate ended the debate by announcing that she couldn't stand waiting a minute longer than was absolutely necessary. She was applying early decision, somewhere.

· · · · · · ·

THEY SAY THE essay is the single most important part of the application. It is the one thing that is truly unique, where the applicant reveals a bit of who she is, how she reacts to the world, and what matters to her.

Since I was a writer, I was only too happy to offer my assistance in this endeavor. She should write about Iraq and Afghanistan to show her knowledge of current affairs. She should do more than send a portfolio of her art; she should write about it and turn her art into words.

She rejected everything I suggested. Instead, she wrote about herself—why she practiced yoga for two hours a day seven days a week, how it felt to drink a cappuccino at a sidewalk café in Paris. She explained how she had come to choose this place, Connecticut College in New London, a former women's college most people in California had never heard of. She wrote about how impressed she was with the college's new center for art and technology, and how she liked the large number of foreign students on campus and the even larger number of domestic students who went abroad to study. New London may not have been the sophisticated urban center of her dreams, but it was only a short train ride to New York, Boston, or Providence.

What really won her heart, she admitted, was the view from campus of Long Island Sound. Without it, New England would be just too claustrophobic for a girl from California who needed a large body of water and a big horizon stretched out before her.

· · · · · · ·

OH GREAT, I thought, she's going to come off as the quintessential California girl. They'll be making L.A. jokes around the admissions table all winter. But when I finally sat down and read the entire application, I was astonished. I had no idea how fascinating and engaging this daughter of mine had become. This was a young woman who had everything going for her; she was a force to contend with. There was no way any college admissions committee would pass on this one, not even one that had turned down 67 percent of its applicants the year before.

Exhausted, I didn't bother to organize applications to other colleges so she could get them out quickly in the unlikely event she was deferred or turned down. I told her not to worry about getting additional recommendation forms to her teachers. She'd hear from Connecticut College on December 15; her high school didn't close for Christmas vacation until December 19. Even if the worst happened, she would still have four days to pull everything together.

·······

THE LETTER WAS late. We had expected it before the weekend, a little ahead of schedule. Some colleges send out acceptances and rejections online, but this was coming the old-fashioned way, by post. The weekend dragged by, then Monday's mail came: nothing. It would definitely be in Tuesday's mail, only it wasn't.

I finally called. There'd been a computer glitch. We'd probably get it Wednesday. We didn't. I called again. Could they tell us on the phone? No, it was on its way. It would be there. When it wasn't, I panicked. One day left. Everyone would be gone from the high school. If Connecticut had decided to say no, we'd miss the January 1 deadline to apply anywhere else.

An admissions officer at the college kindly said she would extend a professional courtesy if Kate's high school college counselor would give her a call. We still hadn't met the college counselor. My daughter had managed to enlist the help of the assistant principal, who had graciously filled out her forms, written a glowing personal recommendation, and seen to it that an official transcript was sent. Now we needed him to call Connecticut College to learn Kate's fate.

Sorry, his secretary said when I called. He was gone. He'd left for vacation a day early. Awful thoughts exploded in my head. I had surely destroyed any chance my daughter had of ever getting into college. I frantically tried to think of a way out. How about taking a year off? Go to Afghanistan and build hospitals.

I phoned the school secretary again, and she reluctantly agreed to call the college herself. Five minutes later she called back and said she couldn't do it.

"You didn't call?" I cried.

"I did call. I just can't tell you what they said."

"What do you mean, you can't tell me? You *have* to tell me."

"I can't. They told me not to tell anyone. The answers come in the mail."

"So what am I supposed to do about getting the recommendation forms to all the teachers and figuring out who can fill out all the official school forms?"

There was a pause.

"Throw them away," she advised.

"That means she is in? Is she? Are you sure?" I was on the verge of tears.

There was another pause. Then, choosing her words carefully, she said: "I'm sure you don't have to do anything with those forms."

· · · · · · · ·

A FEW WEEKS later, I took the round table back to the garden, moved the library table back where it belonged, and stripped everything off the bulletin board before returning it to my office. I stuffed all the old brochures into shopping bags and stowed them in some mildewed cabinets. The family room looked bare so I went to Crate & Barrel and bought a new chair. I realized afterward it was a peculiar acquisition for a family that was about to have one less person around.

I talk to Gracie now and again. Sometimes she makes noises about wanting the crates back. I guess she figures her husband is getting old enough that he doesn't remember where they came from. They live all the way across the country, so I assume she won't collect them anytime soon. The truth is, I still need the crates because the mail hasn't stopped. In fact, it's starting to pick up again. But now some of the envelopes are addressed to a different person. I told you, didn't I, that we have another daughter? Rachel will be a senior in the fall. She's more the scientific type. These marketing people the colleges use are really good because they've already picked up on that. She's getting mailers from very different places than her sister did. One came from MIT just the other day. "We helped get a man on the moon," it read. "We should be able to help you finance your education." Now wouldn't that be nice?

Postscript

BEFORE SHE HAD finished her first semester of college, Kate decided she wanted a more urban campus. She also wanted to study medieval history and religion. Without parental assistance, she applied and was admitted to several universities. Her sophomore year, she transferred to Brown University and spent a semester studying at Universitat de Barcelona. She graduated from Brown in the spring of 2008 with a degree in visual art. She moved to Brooklyn and, after a two-year hiatus from school, is preparing to apply to doctorate programs in art history.

Her sister Rachel filled out her college applications in her father's office, without help from her mother. She attended Northwestern University and graduated in the spring of 2009 with a degree in creative nonfiction writing. She now works for a well-known test prep company, teaching the SAT to low-income high school students. She plans to apply to law school.

A Piece of Cake

·······

Jan Brogan

My firstborn was a quiet and studious child whose high school identity was wrapped up in academics. That she might get sucked into the vortex of the college admissions process was not a shock.

But I believed the second time around would be easier. My son, two and a half years younger, was the easygoing one. My slacker. A guitar player who fronted the rock-and-roll band and got arrested his junior year for drinking beer in the Applebee's parking lot.

His expectations were lower. Ours were lower. A piece of cake.

But I underestimated not just my son, but the pure power of competition.

·······

MY HUSBAND, BILL, and I were typical baby boomers who fell prey to the mistakes of our generation. We had only two children and we focused too intensely on them. We bought all the early childhood education books and did everything they said. I harped on grades, my husband coached sports, and together, we overprotected.

But the one thing we didn't do was pressure our children about college selection. Bill had shuffled through three schools before he wound up graduating from UMass, Boston. I had gone to Boston University mostly because my brother went there.

We also had an overriding concern. Our daughter, Lannie, was a sensitive soul who staved off all possible forms of criticism by making sure she did everything right all the time. At least once every school year, she worked herself into a state of physical exhaustion that mimicked mono. By her freshman year, I was buying books about perfectionism. All of them advocated de-emphasizing the college selection process.

This was especially important because we lived in the kind of affluent suburb known for its school system. The kind of town where parents riot if the high school drops an Advanced Placement class. And where everyone knows exactly how many seniors trot off each year to the Ivy League.

"You know," Bill, a native Minnesotan, would say at the dinner table, "in the Midwest, people don't even talk about Harvard and Yale. They don't understand this obsession Easterners have with the Ivy League."

He talked up the many terrific schools all across the country. The Universities of Michigan, Wisconsin, and Minnesota, where we figured a rare New Englander might have a better chance. He plugged the University of Massachusetts, where he'd gotten "a fine education." I lobbied for McGill University because I thought it would be fun to go to college in Montreal.

The point, we tried to make, was that there were any number of good schools where our kids could be happy. "Just don't get your heart set on any one of them."

After her own methodical search process, Lannie ignored every one of our recommendations. She chose one college as her live-or-die favorite and applied early decision. Another parent actually counseled me not to tell anyone her choice, implying that this would minimize the town-wide gossip and the humiliation of rejection. We spent an entire month not breathing, terrified our firstborn wouldn't be able to cope if she did not get her own way.

But we were lucky. She got in. The worst, we thought, was over.

· · · · · · · ·

OUR SON DID not over-identify with his academic performances. In middle school, he took pains to distance himself from his sister, warning teachers that they were "nothing alike."

And it was true. While she prided herself on her organizational skills, Spike claimed the world's sloppiest locker. In his freshman year, he was renowned for never bringing a pencil or pen to class. At least once a semester I got at least one call from an aggravated teacher about his forgetfulness and the frayed and crumpled homework he turned in.

Even later, when he began to focus more on grades, Spike never hung out with the "smart crowd." A man of the people, my son befriended drinkers and stoners alike. His inner circle went back to elementary school, his friends chosen for loyalty and their unique sense of humor. In a town where

98 percent of the senior class matriculated to college, one of his best friends was planning to make his career in the pipe-fitter's union instead.

But after Spike's trip to juvenile court early his junior year, he had to report regularly to a probation officer. Wisely, she treated him as a lowlife. This shook his suburban self-image to the core. Since he was grounded for three months, and there wasn't much else he could do, Spike decided to study.

Next thing I knew, he was asking me to sign up for an SAT prep course. Then he actually attended all the classes and did the homework. I suspect that it was in these weekly classes, held in the center of the local strip mall, where the real competition began, where the seniors compared their practice test scores and traded their vast knowledge of which schools were worthy and which weren't.

Soon Spike was on Amazon.com, ordering the up-to-date *Fiske Guide to Colleges* and The Princeton Review's *The Best 361 Colleges*. Without a real major or field of study in mind, and with no preferences for school size or location, Spike had no firm guides for whittling down the choices. His only leaning—and we weren't sure why—seemed to be toward Catholic colleges.

One day, I began thumbing through the Princeton Review guide and flipped open to a small Catholic college in New England, which looked genuinely appealing.

"Mom, that's a stoner school."

As if half of his friends weren't stoners.

"A safety," I suggested.

"I'd rather not go to college at all," he said, as if he'd spent years on that campus and couldn't tolerate another day of it.

Later, we visited a school in Georgia that had captured his interest. It was a beautiful day that emphasized a climate much superior to our own. But Spike took an instant dislike to the architecture and the fact that there were fast-food franchises right on campus.

This despite his love of all food McDonald's.

We drove six hours to a small, exclusive school in upper New York State that he rejected on the sole grounds that another boy in our tour group was a typecast preppy, with long blond hair and flip-flops, who kept asking about the squash team. Spike wouldn't even stay for the informational session.

Midway through this process, my son decided that school spirit was critical to him. He wanted to bond with others at football games, so he focused on Notre Dame and Boston College. We flew out to Indiana, where the entire family fell in love with the campus. Later I took Spike to see BC, twenty minutes from our home.

Despite very definitive language on both their Web sites explaining that for late-blooming students like Spike applying early action was a disadvantage, he applied to both colleges early action.

He was deferred.

He tore up each deferral letter immediately after opening it. Then he sulked off to the family room.

"It's not like you were rejected," I called after him.

No response.

"And didn't you say you knew Notre Dame was a long shot?" He moped for two days.

I couldn't stand it, this devastation. Spike was my confident child—the one who had never fretted over a low grade or a coach who didn't like him. He tended to react to setbacks practically, taking action rather than wallowing in emotion. He had stoically endured a traumatic accident on the basketball court the previous season, and toughed his way through reconstructive knee surgery and rehabilitation without complaint. But now, he was all gloom.

"This is all about status," I told him. "About what people think."

He ignored me.

"There are kids who deal with a cancer diagnosis better than this."

He gave me a long, cold look. "Are you calling me a wuss?"

I gave him a cold look back. "I guess I am."

Although he stormed off in another huff, within a half hour, he was himself again, laughing and cracking jokes.

But the deferrals made him wary.

Justly criticized by his teachers for a mind-boggling lack of organization, Spike took on the task of applying to eight other colleges: one more reach, four targets, and three safeties. To appease his sister, who insisted that he'd have a sibling advantage at her college, he made a last-minute addition. The new total of applications was eleven. I'm a writer and he didn't seek my help on any of his half-dozen essays. The only thing he asked was that I write the checks.

· · · · · · ·

AFTER THE JANUARY 1 deadline, Spike seemed back to his old self. It was basketball season, he played center. He was consumed with practices, games, and a myriad of senior events.

Holy Cross sent a letter saying they would welcome additional materials. Spike was a good writer with impressive papers. "Send them one," I suggested.

He blew me off. "Oh, I'll get in somewhere," he replied.

There was only one small problem. He was having trouble eating.

After every meal, his stomach ached. The pediatrician ran blood tests that revealed nothing. He recommended Prilosec and Zantac. Nothing worked.

The gastroenterologist pediatric specialist was able to rule out lactose intolerance and other food allergies. Since Spike's stomach started bothering him only months after his knee surgery, the doctor thought the stomach problems could be a result of all the antibiotics given while he was on the operating table.

But two separate courses of acidophilus—the regular kind and the special refrigerated kind I had to drive two towns away to buy—didn't repopulate his stomach with the "good" bacteria. Or if they did, it didn't relieve the pain. Spike was all set for more intrusive tests that required a trip to the hospital when the gastroenterologist happened to remark: "You know, I get an awful lot of high school seniors in here with these stomach ailments."

So we held off. And it occurred to me that despite his seemingly calm exterior, maybe Spike was just the tiniest bit pent up.

When he received notice that he was eligible for a scholarship at UMass, one of his safety schools, I pinned it to the bulletin board in the kitchen and tried to establish this as a victory. "So the worst-case scenario now is that you go to UMass for free," I said.

Spike gave me a cold look and marched off to the desk in the family room. He returned waving a military recruitment letter at me. "If the only college I get into is UMass," he informed me, "I'm going to apply to the *army* instead."

For a child who had never once asked for a toy gun or a toy soldier, Spike said this with a startling ferocity.

In other words, he'd rather risk his life in Iraq than deal with the lack of status associated with attending the same college his father proudly called his alma mater.

And that's when I realized exactly how much Spike was suffering. He was suffering so badly that he had to raise the stakes for me and make certain that until those life-altering envelopes arrived, I suffered as much as he did.

Not surprisingly, when the first official acceptance came in, Spike's stomach problems disappeared. Out of eleven schools, ten accepted him. Only his first choice, Notre Dame, let him down.

But by then, he didn't care anymore. And despite the fact that he was "nothing like his sister," he was accepted at the same college. Thrilled, he wound up attending a school he hadn't read up on, hadn't officially toured, and where—at least up until his junior year—he wouldn't attend a single football game.

The funny thing about it is that he is supremely happy. And his very best friend plays college squash.

Part 3

. . . .

From the Insiders

Impersonating Wallpaper

The Dean's Daughter Speaks

. . . .

Jennifer Delahunty and Emma Britz

My bright and cheery office on the first floor of the admissions building has many windows and is ideal for watching visitors arrive at our college. Unfortunately, my windows cut most people off around the neck. My daily view is a parade of student and parent heads, parents in the lead 90 percent of the time. With furrowed brows, thinning hair, and cheeks giving way to gravity, these parents carry the weight of the college selection process in their worried eyes. They want the best for their sons or daughters. They want the best for themselves. After all, the fat envelope is a kind of report card for parenting, isn't it? I wish the answer were a definitive "no."

The college search process is so front-loaded with expectation that even those of us who do this for a living approach it with trepidation. I was a brand-new college dean when my oldest daughter, Emma, began her college search. I was delighted when her best friend's mother volunteered to take the two of them to California to look at schools. Emma returned from that trip saying, "It's not really my kind of place, I'm not a warm-weather person. I don't really like wearing shorts." Okay, so college choice was, in part, about the wardrobe? This I hadn't anticipated.

Let me explain my mom's reaction to my admittedly simplistic response. That trip was never about school. It was about hanging out with my best friend and seeing California. Placating my mother by making her think I was giving serious thought to the looming college selection deadline was just an added bonus. Despite what my mom remembers, the trip did teach me what I did not want in my future school. Relaying these thoughts to my mother was, of course, done in cryptic teenage-girl language. Anyone with teenagers knows what I'm talking about. Let me decipher:

"It's not really my place" means "going to a school where the student population is larger than my hometown is terrifying to me."

"I'm not a warm-weather person" actually means "I don't think I'll be able to handle the temptations of the parties, concerts, football games, and the opportunities to 'study' by the pool."

"I don't like wearing shorts" was a mom-friendly way of letting her know that I would never do homework because I would always be at the beach. My report was summarized in two short sentences intended to be so blunt that my mother could not argue with my "reasoning."

. . . .

I WAS DELIGHTED when another friend's mother volunteered to take Emma east to look at colleges. She returned from that trip saying, "I don't like that much competition." So college choice was also about the perceived psychic toll antici-pated on any given college campus. Emma was never that competitive, but it didn't seem like a good reason for crossing off an entire region of the country.

"Too competitive" translates to "these students already have the next twenty years of their lives planned out." I didn't know what I wanted to major in, let alone where I wanted to get my first job out of college. These kids already figured out all the de-tails between high school graduation and receiving their advanced degrees a decade later. It was daunting and I definitely did not fit that mold.

With both the East and West Coasts crossed off the list, I now had to face the fact that I had not slithered out from un-der the responsibility of the college tour. I was going to have to get into the car and take my furrowed brow and my daugh-ter to a few college campuses.

Emma and I started our tour on a liberal arts campus where we were informed that students were paid a quarter for def-ecating into a compost toilet. When Emma heard that this same school had no physical education requirement, she said, "Sign me up."

This blunt response was intended to tease my visibly shocked mother. I changed my mind after I learned this same school proudly celebrated "Cape Day." Sure, I liked Harry Potter, but not that much.

We sat through an information session and then she did her first interview. When we got into the car, she said, "Why aren't you asking any questions?" I informed her that I was a dean undercover. I didn't want to shape her expectations by asking any of the questions I knew to ask ("What is the

freshman to sophomore retention rate?" or "How many faculty live within a half hour of campus?"). I wanted this to be
her experience entirely, but I knew that she was watching me
for clues. It's not easy to impersonate wallpaper, but I was
working very hard at it.

We proceeded to what I thought would be the perfect
school for her—one with strong international programs in a
dynamic small city. We drove for hours across a Midwestern
state only to arrive in the middle of a late autumn snowstorm.
As we got out of the car, I looked down at Emma's yellow
flip-flops. "Is that all you brought to wear on your feet?" She
nodded. We did the chilly tour and afterward, she declared
there was no sense of community on campus. I wanted to shout,
"You clearly have hypothermia!" but I didn't. I resumed my
wallpaper pose.

*I wasn't freezing, I just had an immediate dislike for the school
and I couldn't quite pinpoint why. It didn't help that the students
looked unfriendly and unhappy, even in their closed-toed shoes.*

And so it went. What about this campus? "Too jock-y," she
pronounced.

*Too much emphasis on sports can be bad. It creates a social
hierarchy.*

And this one? "Too nerdy."

*The kids needed to have social lives; I didn't want to go some-
where with only "indoor kids."*

Her impressions visceral, her statements superficial, Emma
responded with her gut—which she clearly had good access
to—after every stop on the campus tour trail. I admired her
decisiveness but worried about how quickly she limited her
options.

On these tours my go-to question was, "Why did you choose this school?" No one said, "Oh, because it has a great freshman to sophomore retention rate." Instead, I almost always received the same answer about how their school just felt right to them. I knew my decision wouldn't be based on an informational session or statistic. I was looking for that feeling everyone kept talking about.

The parent's role in this whole odyssey is so ill-defined that we end up feeling like something between a taxi driver and a walking checkbook. You are bankrolling the initial journey—the Starbucks stops, as well as the pricey plane tickets—and you'll be responsible for the big ticket at the end, but in the meantime, it's like taking a toddler to buy a car. Let's be honest: When choosing a college, our children don't really know what they're looking for. They have not yet, after all, had to stay up all night to write a treatise on *Howard's End*, faced the devastation of a biology experiment gone bad, nor experienced that epiphanic moment as they delved into another culture. They don't know that the friends they make in college will shape not only their musical tastes, but the lens through which they see the world. And maybe—just maybe—this is all for the better.

I knew exactly what I was looking for in a college. When it came down to it, I recognized that all the schools had fantastic academic reputations, and I would get a great education at any one of them. Having assumed that much, I focused on the little things like academic requirements, the meal plan, whether students stayed on campus during the weekends, how many speakers and musicians came to school, and, of course, what the students were like. Parents don't give us enough credit; I knew that the students walking by me on those tours would shape my life and the way I see the world. That's why I was so picky.

· · · · · · ·

EMMA APPLIED TO four colleges—all Midwestern, of varied levels of selectivity. I took one look at her essay (no pens allowed!) and asked one question. She actually listened and reshaped the ending . . . then pushed the keys to transport all her applications into the various in-boxes of those colleges that didn't get the "too this" or "too that" pronouncement. I sighed a little too loudly as I watched her push the keys. "What's wrong?" she asked. I had no answer.

We waited and we watched the mail arrive. The postcards and envelopes that clogged our mailbox remained mostly ignored on the kitchen table. Whenever I handed her a piece of mail during a meal at that table, she just said, "Whatever," and shrugged.

It sounds like I didn't care. Really, though, Mom just didn't get my strategy. Yes, there was a strategy: Know enough about the schools to want to be accepted, but not enough to get your heart set on any one. Once you've been accepted, learn more about the school and then, only then, is it acceptable to become more emotionally invested. I would not be one of those kids crying over the thin envelope.

All those carefully crafted messages were lost on Emma. If she only knew how much of *my* life was spent attending to those messages. But then again, I was reading them—and if I was reading them, so were parents across America. We are the taxi drivers and the financiers, yes, but also the "Consumer Report" for our college-searching sons and daughters. We care too deeply *not* to read the mail addressed to our sons and daughters.

The ironic thing about that period of waiting was that I too was keeping thousands of students waiting. I was evaluating applications in my office and one of them happened to be my daughter's. Because of the way we read in my office, however, I wasn't assigned her application. Whew. I was, however, aware of the day she came to interview with one of my colleagues. After Emma left the building, the colleague sauntered into my office and declared her a "neat kid." Was that code for something? I became like every other parent in this process—paranoid and, quite frankly, a little anxious. Still, I didn't look at her record in our computer system nor check her interview write-up.

In our admission decision process at Kenyon, two officers read every application. If both readers agree, a decision has been reached. If the readers disagree or are unsure, the file goes to committee and ten officers sit around a seminar table and discuss the strengths and weaknesses of the candidate. We do this in state order. It takes us a day or more to evaluate Ohio split-decision applications, and I didn't actually know the verdict on my daughter's candidacy until we were sitting in committee and I saw "admit" next to her name. My efforts to remain in the background paid off. I hadn't even seen her full application and it had made it to the pile slated to receive the fat envelope. I let the wallpaper imitation slip away and said beneath my breath, "Yeah!" I might have even pumped my fist under the table.

On the day the decisions were to be placed in the mail, the staff handed me the acceptance envelope—a sweet, emotion-filled moment for me. My first daughter was being invited to join my first admitted class. I brought it home, stuck it in the mailbox, and sent her out to get the day's mail. She came back into the house with a sly smile. "Kenyon," she said, holding the big, white envelope. She sat down at the kitchen table and then began reading everything in the packet. At last, she was reading the material!

With her father at the wheel this time, she returned to the other schools where she had been admitted. She really liked a Wisconsin college, but commented warily, "The students are kinda weird." I wanted to shout at the top of my nearly half-century-old lungs, "Yes, they're smart and quirky and so are you—it's perfect!" But knowing that what I said about that college, or any college, would carry little weight, I bit my tongue, which was mighty sore by mid-April.

In the last week of April, she tapped on the door of my office. She came in, a bit slumped beneath her backpack. "Mom," she said, taking a deep breath. "I've decided to go to Kenyon." Now, *this* was news. This kid had spent ten months in Argentina at age sixteen as an AFS exchange student. Ten months during which I didn't see her face. This kid had tried every activity under the sun and settled on the riskier activities as her hobbies. Wait—this adventurous kid who had always pushed at the barriers was now choosing the familiar? She must have seen the question mark above my head.

"It's just that I feel I can get the most accomplished here," she said, the embodiment of matter-of-fact.

When I applied to the other schools, I decided there was no way I would ever go to Kenyon. Come on, my mom was the dean. Then, I revisited each of my four schools for an overnight visit and each one was tentatively crossed off my list for one reason or another. Kenyon was the last one I visited. I stayed in the dorms and couldn't get over how much I liked everyone I met. We didn't even do anything that exciting. We stayed in, did homework, and ordered late-night quesadillas from the local grill. I finally got that feeling I was looking for, the one everyone kept talking about. I was comfortable there even as a "prospie," and I felt like this was where I belonged.

Regardless of how casual my mom makes all of this sound, I weighed my pros and cons very carefully before I made my final decision. I really only had one "con" on my list: As my mom said, I was an adventurous kid choosing the familiar. I would be going to school closer, much closer, to home than I ever thought I would. This meant I would probably see my parents more often than the average American college student. I decided this was a mixed blessing and that it was no reason not go to the college where I felt like I belonged.

Students choose colleges for all sorts of reasons. I chose the school I attended because someone nice handed me a pencil in the class I was visiting and said, "You'll want to take notes." Choosing the familiar because she felt she could get the most accomplished—now, this *was* a darn good reason to choose a college.

My daughter has graduated from college and has marched successfully into her "real" life. She has accomplished much, but perhaps her biggest accomplishment, not even on her agenda, was to show her mother, the dean, that kids end up where they should, regardless of anything we do in admissions or anything that transpires across the kitchen table.

I am grateful my mother tried to impersonate wallpaper during my search. She didn't pressure, discourage, or share favorites. She gave me room to breathe and figure out what I wanted in my future school. But I knew she was there if I ever wanted to talk about my search. It's important for parents to let their kids go through the college process at their own pace and in their own way. At times, it may look like kids are disinterested and not taking the search seriously, but most likely, the wheels in their heads are turning a million miles a minute. My mom didn't understand the reasons that I liked some schools and not others, but in the end, she held to her wallpaper role and let me trust my gut. You may not understand the reasons why your sons and daughters choose the schools they do, but trust them to know what they're looking for and they'll make the right decision.

A Life of Too Much

·······

Lisa Gates

Getting to college really shouldn't be this stressful. I know the applicant numbers are way up and the acceptance rates are way down. I know parents are seeking out all kinds of help for their kids—from expensive SAT prep courses to far more expensive private counselors—in order to strengthen and package the college application in just the right way. I know places that used to be safety schools aren't such a safe bet any longer, and even the state university is suddenly competitive. When I applied to colleges some twenty-five years ago, it didn't seem all that hard. I visited campuses and picked my favorites based on location, architecture, and the presence of the opposite sex. I took the SATs—twice, in fact, trying to get that math score up without the aid of a class. I wrote some essays, sent the applications off in the mail, and waited anxiously for the fat envelopes in April.

Clearly things have changed in college admissions, but oddly enough, as I begin the process with my oldest child, I find myself helping him do pretty much what I did. Which is to say, take the standardized tests, find schools that seem like a good match based on his interests—and my own in paying the tuition bill—and get the applications together.

You might find this approach quaint or radically deluded, but there's a reason for it. I've been in higher ed my whole life, it seems, starting at the age of seventeen when I packed my bags for college. I've studied, worked, and taught at large research universities, public and private, and small liberal arts colleges—all of them in that group of schools flooded with applications each year. I know the magical, the good, the bad, and the ugly of higher ed. And I know it does not matter where my son goes to college. His life is in his own hands, even if he doesn't fully understand that yet.

I went off to college in a more laissez-faire time when there were pay phones in the hallway, beer pong was a primary social activity, and friends with privileges meant you could borrow their car. Don't get me wrong: Dartmouth in the mid-1980s was hardly an idyllic place for a young woman, particularly one with feminist sentiments. But unless you were in serious trouble with your grades or the judicial board, you were pretty much left alone. What you did, what you made of yourself there, was largely a result of your own initiative and the students and faculty with whom you connected.

And parents back then? That was what the pay phone was for—the weekly check-in.

Today it's a different story. The parents I see around me are so deeply invested in their children, their support and monitoring takes on a life of its own. We all know parents who check the homework nightly, ferry the forgotten instrument or book or sports equipment to school, or call the teacher to complain about a grade. The ones who drive an hour out of their way so that a son or daughter can attend the "right" school. Folks who send their kids to the camp two states away or get them on the competitive travel team so their kid might be noticed by a D-I college coach. Or who use their vacation money to send a high schooler on a community service trip to Guatemala. I know mothers who pack their teens' lunches every morning and make their breakfast. And I confess I have my own moments of weakness, staying up late to wash the track uniform because I had just been informed of a re-scheduled meet, and really, my son needed the sleep. After all, I just had to go to work the next day. No one was expecting me to run the 800 meters in under 2:10.

But we all know these parents. They are our friends and neighbors and ourselves to greater or lesser degrees. What we do is an extension of our love for our children: We want them to have every advantage, especially the ones we didn't have. We want them to excel and have the opportunity to focus on their talents and their academics. We don't want them to suf-fer, and if we can help them avoid it, why shouldn't we? But the result is we've created a whole generation of young people who are so well cared for and so overly dependent on us, they lack fundamental and necessary skills in solving problems, handling disappointment, and making difficult choices. And those last bits, in a nutshell, come in pretty handy in college.

Forget the rhetoric in the admissions brochure about edu-cating leaders of the next generation. How will a young per-son ever negotiate a resolution to a global conflict if they have to call Mom or Dad to figure out a roommate problem? How will they have the courage to take chances in their lives if every small choice is first vetted with Mom or Dad? How will you slog through the ups and downs of work life if you call home in tears when the only section of Spanish that works for your schedule is full? How will these kids manage a bad decision or a disappointment if they never have any experience sorting through the consequences of their choices? How will they ever learn to speak up for themselves if Mom or Dad is the one calling me about the student's problem? The cell phone and Internet have done wonders for our ability to stretch the umbilical cord. At one meeting, I heard a psychiatrist at an Ivy League school tell the story of a student whose parent called every night to read her a story before bed. *Ouch.* This support, this coddling, has got to end sometime. And it should have ended long before the kids arrive for first-year orientation.

In my first years as a dean, I was often surprised by the kind of young men and women who ended up in my office. I expected to see some students from disadvantaged backgrounds, students for whom the academic rigor or the distance from home, or the experience of being surrounded by such wealth, could be a difficult adjustment. I expected some students with disabilities and health issues that affected their ability to get their work done. But the ones who surprised me were the students who had had every advantage—and therein lay the problem. Without the constant monitoring and propping up by the parents and the resources they marshaled for their kids—the private schools, pricey college counselors, therapists, coaches—their kids fell apart. These were kids who had no experience with failure, because parents or their extensive support system had never let it happen. Once they're at college, though, small issues can become much more serious and their utter surprise at the seriousness of their predicaments is, well, surprising.

Take class attendance, for example. At a residential college, faculty really do require students to attend and participate in class in order to pass. Seems reasonable, really, and if you're the one paying that tuition bill, you probably agree it's a good thing. Even so, some students regularly have problems with that requirement. I once had a student who was at risk of failing an art class. Because it was a studio class, you had to be there to do the work. But it was a Monday, Wednesday, Friday morning class, and she regularly overslept. The student insisted she loved the class, refused to drop it because it was so great, and so I worked out a contract with the course instructor that if, and only if, she attended all remaining classes for the semester, she could pass. But then right after spring break, she missed class again. She came to my office with a handwritten note from her father, explaining the circumstances. She had been on a fabulous European holiday with her family and their return flight really couldn't be changed to accommodate her class schedule. Would I please explain to her art teacher?

Clearly students like this have some problem—or likelier, several problems—that interfere with their ability to get their work done. But I do think in part it stems from a life of too much: too much help, too much hovering, too much control from those who love them most. So when these students are suddenly confronted with the demands of college—organizing and managing their time, finding help when it's needed, speaking up for themselves—they are at a loss.

The result for me, as a parent, is that I'm probably harder

on my kids than many of my peers. If my son complains about a problem in a class, I tell him to talk to the teacher. Problem on the soccer field? Talk to the coach. If he's unsure about which SAT tests he should take and when he should take them, I tell him to go to Guidance and look online. He's hoping to take a French class at the college near us, since his high school won't offer the class he needs. I told him to e-mail the professor. Of course I will read the e-mail if he asks. I make suggestions, things he could do and what the possible outcome might be if he does or doesn't do those things. I do this because he is sixteen and because he needs to learn how to think through problems and advocate for himself. And what better place for him to learn than here and now, before he leaves for college?

Because the reality is, life happens all the time on our campuses. Students may discover their academic skills aren't quite up to par for college work. They may need to choose between completing a double major and studying abroad. Or they may have to sacrifice time in theater to pass a Chinese language course. Or need to accept the consequences of failing a class. But those are the little things, I tell them. You work through the consequences and move forward. The big things happen here too, things that are life-shaping and life-altering. I have worked with some remarkable young people over the years: a first-generation, full-scholarship student at the top of her class wins a fellowship to graduate school. A young gay man from a conservative, religious family, struggles with his double life— out on campus, hiding at home—and is certain that if he tells them, the family he loves will disown him. A young transgendered woman begins the process of living as a man. A student has to leave school when recreational drug use turns into something more insidious. A classmate dies after getting horribly drunk and wandering out into the night. A brother is killed in Afghanistan. These things happen—the good, the bad, the magical, and the horrible.

It is hard for me not to react to this and do what I can to prepare my son, not just for college, but for life, which as I have known it is not always fair or happy, but can be filled with moments of great joy. I want him to know love and passion, to find work that is important to him, and to find a community, a family in addition to the one he has now, that he cares for and who care for him. I also want him to learn how to handle disappointment and failure and learn how to persevere when things are difficult. College will be a big part of that process, but *which* college ultimately doesn't matter all that much. Every place I have studied or worked has been filled with faculty and staff who care about the education of these young people. If I teach him how to make responsible decisions, how to plan, how to find the right people to ask for advice, how to accept the consequences of actions—or inaction, as is so often the case in academic disasters!—he will be brilliant at this college business.

So how am I helping him prepare for this process? We've visited a few campuses and taken some tours, so he can start understanding a bit better what college life is like and how these campuses might be different from one another. I'm encouraging him to think about what he likes, what he finds interesting, what he thinks he is good at. I ask him questions: Do you like big or small? Do you want to know every other person you see or every tenth person? What would you like to study? "Not English," has been the consistent response so far. Fine, but what else? Do you want a place strong in science and math and music? Do you want to play soccer? So far, we're looking for a small school in a place warmer than Vermont where he can play soccer, not major in English, and engage in some undergraduate research in the sciences, maybe. I can think of at least forty schools that fill that bill off the top of my head.

Ultimately, there is no perfect place for my son, or for any college applicant, but there are many good ones. There will always be something wrong with them: too small, too remote, too conservative, too weird, or not weird enough. Architecture 101 may always be full, or the dorm rooms crummy. Grad students might teach some of the classes. A famous professor may be past his prime. My advice? Decide what's most important, in broad strokes. What do you want to learn about? What interests do you want to continue or pursue? What sorts of things do you imagine you might like to do with your life? Talk to students about their lives at school. Visit the campus. Spend a night. And by all means, attend a few classes. But remember, once you get to campus, your interests may change. What if biochemistry really isn't your forte and on top of that, you find it boring? What if you take a religion class and it turns you on to something big? What if you're a recruited athlete, but you get injured and spend the season sitting on the sidelines? What if you fall off a mountain and end up in a wheelchair? Things happen. Life happens. We do the best we can to get where we want to go. And with some luck, love, and perseverance, we may get there or maybe somewhere else that's even better.

I am confident my son will have several good schools to choose from when he gets those letters in April of his senior year. Together, we'll look at all the things he said were most important to him—the strength of particular academic programs, the soccer team, the location—as well as the things that matter to me, like the expense, and our collective impressions of the campus and its students and faculty. We'll make a decision, send in the deposit, and deliver him in August. The rest will be up to him. But if I've done my job well, he'll have all he needs to make these years what they should be: intellectually formative, personally enriching, and life-changing. He'll discover why, after all these years of studying and working, I still love college. It's a place where you fall in love: with ideas, with people, with causes. It's where you develop a sense of self and what you are capable of. It's a place where ideas and ideals matter. It's a place of eternal possibility.

The Kids Are Alright

(With Apologies to The Who)

....

Debra Shaver

My entire professional life—over a quarter century—has been spent in the college admission profession, currently as a director. I've also recently experienced the process as a parent of a (at the time only "likely") college-bound son. Since I meet so many overly involved parents, I wanted to avoid that kind of behavior at all costs with my own son. I didn't want the process of getting into college to end up being more mine than his, and I didn't want him to spend his high school years anxiously making every decision based on what would impress an admissions officer. And let me tell you, neither happened.

During my son John's search he expressed interest in a number of post–high school experiences. Early on he announced that he wanted to go to Duke. To play basketball. He wasn't even on the high school team! At five feet tall, I knew no son of mine was playing Division I basketball. He complained that I was crushing his dreams.

Next John announced that he wanted to go to culinary

school. Gosh, that was surprising, since he doesn't cook. "No, but I like to watch you cook and I like to eat. I think culinary school is the perfect match." I was delighted to hear that he was thinking in terms of "match" and not just about getting into the most competitive colleges. He must have listened to some of what I said about the best way to conduct a college search process. When he added that he expected to play baseball in college, so he needed a culinary school with a strong baseball team, I knew we were in trouble.

Junior year John really began thinking about the future. At dinner one night he announced that he had decided that he wasn't going to college because he planned to be a rock star. That's right: rock *star*. "Mom, let me put it in terms you'll understand. I don't expect to be Mick Jagger. I only want to be Keith Richards." What a relief—just the lead guitarist. Couldn't he go to college *and* be a rock star? No, he felt he needed to follow his "passion."

My husband and I decided we were going to proceed as if John was going to college even if he wasn't heading in that direction. The summer before his senior year, we took the requisite family vacation/college visit trip and lo and behold, John found several colleges that he termed both "sick" and "sweet." I'm fairly sure that means "very good" in teen-speak.

In the end, John did go to college. It may not be an Ivy or little Ivy, but it's the right match for him and he loves it. That's what twenty-five years of experience in this profession has taught me. As Roger Daltrey sang, "The kids are alright"—and I would add, wherever they land. John has even broadened his career goals. If the rock star thing doesn't work out, he plans to teach high school history. As long as the record company doesn't call with a contract, I'm confident he'll stay and graduate.

I couldn't be happier—John made it through high school without getting hysterical about getting into college. I'm glad one of us did.

Let It/Them Be

(With or Without Apologies to the Beatles),

or How *Not* to Spend Your
Child's Summer Vacation

. . . .

Katherine Sillin

In March, when families are packing the family vehicle for a week on the college visit circuit, I start to get the phone calls. "What about the summer!?" It's the last frontier on the college application front: how to wow that college admissions officer with a dazzling or different summer adventure. There's almost always a note of panic in the parent's voice. Particularly in recent years, the question of how high school students should spend their summers has taken on a new sense of urgency as this vacation time presents new opportunities to beef up the college application. As the parent of much younger children, this dynamic—even compulsion—has always given me pause, and did especially this past summer.

Yarmouth, where I live, is a charming little town on the southern coast of Maine, about halfway between Portland and L.L.Bean. For residents and visitors alike, it's one of the best (or on the way to the best) coastal destinations come summertime. It's also a place families are drawn to settle because of the outstanding schools, nearby outdoor recreation, and easy access to all that Maine's largest city has to offer. First dibs on the myriad of options offered through Yarmouth Community Services for summer camps is also a great perk that taxpayers enjoy in the summer months. Most people in town are hyperaware of the day that the summer camp bulletin drops in the mail. Even more important is the morning that registration opens.

I'm the kind of parent that is often a step or more behind these types of details, and friends take seriously their perceived responsibility to make sure I'm at least on the cusp of the loop, if not fully in it. I did not have the benefit of this oversight my first spring in Yarmouth. On registration morning I broke out of my office and sauntered over to the Community Services Office, proud that I'd actually remembered the important day. I even stopped for a leisurely cup of coffee along the way. I arrived in time to find myself at the end of a very long, very anxious-looking line. Almost immediately, an acquaintance highlighted my failure to grasp the importance of timing on this critical morning. He then proceeded to share what felt like a collective reality in my town: "Our entire summer depends on this morning."

As educators, my husband and I have the luxury of spending the entire summer largely as we wish with our kids. Many families obviously turn to these wonderful programs as they juggle the same busy work schedules that we do during the school year. This spring about the time those bulletins hit the mail, I stopped to chat with a neighbor who has four

boys and understandably sees the value in providing each
with sufficient productive outlets for their energy. Her days
are largely spent chauffeuring the four from one activity to
the next. She told me that her youngest (age nine) had broken
down in tears that afternoon at the prospect of being dragged
around in the car to each of the other boys' commitments before being dropped off at his own practice. Gulp.

The following week, after discussing all the options with
my kids, I allowed registration day to come and go. None of
the summer programs seemed more exciting to them than
just enjoying the freedom of having no specific plans.

·······

THIS MADE ME think about how I scheduled my own kids
outside of school, and what *their* priorities might be for the
summer ahead. Suddenly I felt even more adamant about
wanting my six- and eight-year-old children to feel the joy of
summer stretching out before them: the thrill of waking up
to a clear, warm, sunny morning and getting out the big De-
Lorme atlas to pick a spot to spend the day. I wanted them to
spend all morning (or even all day, if it was raining!) in their
pajamas playing marathon games of Monopoly if they chose.
I'm surrounded by a sea of overscheduled teens on a daily
basis, and the stress and fatigue that surrounds their lives is
palpable. It makes me more determined to let my kids be kids
for as long as possible—allowing them to take part in defining and creating what is "fun" without always doing it for
them.

Of course there's a balance to be struck, and it is this fact
that I am so consciously aware of in all aspects of helping

guide students and families through the college search and admission process at the small independent school where I work. I'm often asked the question that goes something like: "Which will look better, teaching tennis lessons to eight-year-olds, or volunteering to restore trails in a nearby state park?" I assume they're referring to how all of this will look to the Colleges. My response is almost always the same: "Which do you think your son/daughter would really enjoy doing more—which would he/she find more interesting?" It might not surprise you to know that often the answer is, "Well, D: none of the above." What she'd actually love to do is read for pleasure and practice playing the guitar, or work at the custard stand scooping ice cream with her friends. Not only is this okay, I argue, it's actually more compelling for students to pursue genuine interests in the summer months instead of simply playing to the college admissions crowd and trying to predict what they would find most catchy.

I challenge the students and parents I work with to consider what they value as opposed to how things might look. I encourage them to think more broadly about how they define success (and goodness!)—both in the college admission process, and in life. There is so much emphasis placed on the perceived value of securing a place at a name-brand college or university. Instead, I encourage them to think about which colleges will meet their individual needs and priorities. Which colleges feel like a comfortable match, places that they could see themselves thriving and being happy for four years? Which colleges value the same things that they do? I wonder aloud sometimes if there might be greater fulfillment to be found in striving for happiness on some level as opposed to defining success simply in terms of achievement. The same thing goes for summer plans. Most colleges have come to value authenticity of late, much in the same way that "passion" became the catchphrase a few years back. Contrived summer experiences—no matter how grand—tend to be sniffed out a mile away, particularly if the student involved is ultimately just going through the motions.

Let's be honest, by the time these kids are seniors, many of them have jumped through every hoop imaginable: their own, those provided by the well-meaning parent, and those generally assumed to be destined to impress the college admissions officer. They've attended every camp and every showcase, done some equivalent of Outward Bound, and found time to volunteer at the local soup kitchen—often because there has been a sense that these are the kinds of things that a college will value and that will help them be successful in the college application process. The net result is the fatigue of the over-stressed kid. Some might argue it's the end of that arc that begins with us as parents over-scheduling our young children—not affording them the opportunity to exercise their young imaginations and recharge their batteries, but instead filling their time with organized activities.

The arc moves predictably from over-scheduled youth to the hyper-managed teen to the completely burnt-out senior. I encourage parents to think carefully about the trade-offs. Consider reinforcing true interests and hobbies at any age, even if it may appear that communicating these choices to a college might somehow lack luster. Students don't necessarily need to compete on the premier soccer team or participate in that eco-friendly service-learning opportunity to impress a college admissions officer. Essentially, each student tells a story through their application when they apply to college—a story of who they are and what they value. Shouldn't this whole crazy process be more about finding those places that find that individual story compelling than about how that window sticker is going to look on the back of the car driving through town? The story doesn't necessarily have to contain high drama or Olympic-caliber athletic achievement—just a genuine window to who this seventeen-year-old is at this moment in time. That story tells the college a lot about who this person would be on their campus and how they would contribute in the context of their community.

I encourage the freshmen and sophomores at my school to think carefully about the choices they make as to how they spend their time outside of academic commitments. I challenge them to think in terms of the quality of their experiences as they pursue the things that are truly meaningful to them, and not to focus on the quantity of organizations or clubs that they can list on a résumé come college application time. I even tell them that it's okay to carve out a little breathing room here and there! I tell the students I work with all the time that when it comes to making an impression on a college admissions officer, there is no substitute for communicating what they value most in life with honest and genuine enthusiasm.

I often tell the story of a senior who sat with an admissions officer during a high school visit and was asked to describe how she'd use an hour or two of free time if she actually had it. She closed her eyes and shook her head in a dreamy way and smiled when she said, "I'd sit in the hammock in my backyard and read the next book in this series of historical mystery novels that I started over the summer. Then I'd see what was in the fridge and create something for dinner for my family." It wasn't high literary fiction, and it wasn't some grand adventure, but in that brief moment, this admissions officer got a real glimpse of a few things that really made this student tick.

This past weekend, with summer drawing to a close, we reflected as a family on the high points of our own vacation time together. There were lots of highlights from which to choose: hiking in Acadia, learning to kayak around the island, body surfing at Popham Beach, family camping with friends, swimming with the California cousins—just to name a few. The top memory of our soon-to-be first- and third-grader? Waking up most mornings with no agenda.

Part 4

....

From a Mother's Perspective

The Deep Pool

....

Anna Quindlen

*L*et the record reflect that I was not anyone's idea of happy my first semester of college. I felt out of place socially and outclassed in the classroom, wondering what I had been thinking when I'd picked a hyperintellectual urban hotbed of ambition and second-wave feminism instead of someplace with a leafy green quad and a dedication to theme parties. The freshman fifteen was not an issue; I was so nauseous from homesickness that I lost weight despite the bagels in the cafeteria and the pastrami at the corner deli.

Administrators have asked me to stop telling this story at orientation because it is too depressing for the students. You see, the discombobulated freshman became a driven senior, and that senior became a trustee and eventually chairman of the board of Barnard College. What I will not stop telling the students is this: The place made me what I am today. That's the key to both my service to the college, and my attitude toward how students go about finding a college of their own.

I can only imagine how my mother and father would have responded to my early unhappiness if they'd been the helicopter parents with which most college administrators are familiar today. There's no question there would have been an animated discussion about transferring. In fact I might even have gone elsewhere. My insides freeze when I think about it. My entire life would have been different, from the career path I followed to the family I've created since I met my husband at a Barnard tea.

But in these times there has developed a mythology about falling in love with a college that would have judged my experience an irredeemable disaster. It goes like this: A high school student will go from place to place, pacing the quad, taking the tour, eyeing the students. And one afternoon, in Northampton or Chapel Hill or Palo Alto, her eyes will soften, her mouth will lift, and she will say, "Yes. This is it."

And for four years she will live happily ever after.

Of course deconstructing this mythology means recognizing how preposterous it is. On what do our sons and daughters base their decision? Is it the glittering stretch of limestone, the soft-serve ice cream in the student center, or the students on campus who remind them of . . . them? Best case, it may be a particularly brilliant lecture by a history professor, or a smart and engaging edition of the school humor magazine. All of which may mean nothing if a professor is so popular that it's close to impossible to get into her class, or the graduating magazine editor is replaced by a dud. Occasionally students do get it right, although usually in the rejecting: Our left-of-center son once visited a place at which he thought he would be comfortable and concluded he would never be challenged. "Their motto should be 'We're all different, just like you,' " he said.

The other problem with falling in love is that it doesn't adequately reflect the maturation of individuals in the critical years between seventeen and twenty-two. Students talk sometimes about feeling instantly at home in a place. But is a comfort level what is really called for here? It was actually my discomfort level that made me initially unhappy at Barnard and yet eventually made it a place that took me from the plateau of late adolescence into an adulthood of critical thinking, constant curiosity, and intellectual engagement. In growing into the place, I grew up exponentially. I suspect that if I had chosen a college that felt like home, I wouldn't have felt as capable of being thrust into the world when I was handed my diploma. Or I would have come to feel bored or constrained during my four years. The place that utterly charms a high school senior may feel quite small to a college junior.

Falling in love with a college is like most other *coups de foudre*. Sometimes it flames out fast. Sometimes it lasts. Sometimes it grows into custom and comfort cut with boredom. Perhaps a truly great college choice should be more like an arranged marriage: common background and experiences, with the presumption that affection will develop and grow. I suspect that's what my parents believed about Barnard. They were neither surprised nor alarmed about my early unhappiness: College was a challenging and difficult transition to which it might take some time to accustom myself. I think they would have been perplexed by our current notion that only bliss, day one, was an acceptable mode. Truth is, it perplexes me, and worries me, too. College should be aspirational, designed not to reinforce who a student is but to elevate her to the point at which she dares to be the best self she can become, intellectually and personally. We have to help our sons and daughters realize that they are not looking for a warm bath but a deep pool when they decide where to go to college. That's how they learn to swim.

When Love Gets in the Way

·······

Jane Hamilton

*W*hen the future college boy was in his swaddling clothes I would never have dreamed that a girlfriend—a *girlfriend*—would be the weighty factor in the college choice. Already this baby had a fund, made possible by both sets of grandparents; already he had the good fortune to be a legacy going back several generations, not just at one college but at three venerable institutions. There was evidence in the gene pool that he'd probably be qualified to matriculate at a small liberal arts college, the type of school my husband and I felt had given us deep experiences and our dearest friends. And, although we'd gone to different schools, the connections we'd made during those years had led us to each other. In fact, we needed to pass down to our children the small liberal arts college the way some parents must see to it that their offspring are born again. We didn't care about the job market, about technical real-life skills: College was about becoming the people they were supposed to be, about having loving and mildly draconian professors challenge them, and finding joy.

Under our son's lucky, silver-spoon circumstances, it seemed all he had to do was grow up doing the usual college-bound tasks, and he would have excellent choices.

The love that began early on in his high school career ran so deep he broke the heirloom walnut bedroom door with his bare hands when we forbade him to go to her house every night until 10:00 P.M. It was a fearsome thing, that rage, that passion. We hadn't understood, until then, the force of his feeling. "Wow," my husband said. We dimly remembered maybe having felt something of the sort decades before. As far as the college-bound tasks, there were the problems that often come along with adolescent boys. He didn't always live up to his academic potential, he was occasionally mouthy, he had some trouble with authority, he stayed up way too late in the online gaming universe, and he didn't always seem to grasp the consequences of his every action. Looking back now, he was a remarkably easy teenager, a delight, but at the time we fretted.

Every summer my college friends and I gathered for a week at my grandmother's lake house with our children, and so in their high school years we had the luxury of fretting together about the application process. Would they get in, what more should be done to ensure their getting in, what were admissions people really looking for, how much should we interfere? One July, when we again were sitting around in the living room rehashing our questions, my son's girlfriend looked up at us from her book and said, "Is that all you think about? The small liberal arts college? That's all you've been talking about for days. That's all you've been talking about for years."

She had every reason to think we were cracked. Sometimes, I think we probably were insane. We were, at the least, obsessed. As the senior year sped to application time I became feverish with worry. The girlfriend was going to a small state school. She was a hard worker, she was focused, she knew what she wanted to study, she understood what financial support she had and what loans she had to take out, and she made her choice early. My son applied to my college, his father's college, his grandfather's college, his girlfriend's college, and a well-respected small liberal arts university thirty miles from her school: no one's college. He was admitted to each one. Our choices for him, either his father's school or my school, had national reputations and were out of state. He indulged us by visiting them. Twice we went to scope out the girlfriend's school and the nearby university. He was so happy walking around the state school grounds, no doubt thinking of their future together.

On the second of those trips, we had a terrific fight in the car. I suppose I had been trying to suppress my feelings, and therefore I was making inane comments. I said at one point that I liked the number of deciduous trees on the university campus, whereupon he noted that the state school also had a fine level of *deciduosity*. Finally he cried out, "WHY CAN'T YOU JUST SAY WHAT YOU REALLY WANT ME TO DO?" And I screamed back, "I DON'T WANT YOU TO GO TO THE STATE SCHOOL."

"Thank you," he said.

"You're welcome," I replied.

We next discussed why I didn't want him to go to her school. I'm sure I mentioned in veiled and unveiled ways, at various decibel levels as befits the crone stage of life, key points such as: His relationship wouldn't last, and then what? And, every single person at the state school was blond and half of them were commuters. And, if he went there it would be quite like high school—a few stellar teachers struggling against the exercise in mediocrity.

In the end he chose the small university, a choice that— both dependent on and independent of the girlfriend's proximity—was perfect for him. It didn't come with any of his relatives' accomplishments, it was unheralded and humble, it didn't smell of money, and it was first-rate. During his four years, among many other things, he read Alice Munro stories, he took studio art, he studied Buddhism, he worked on robotics during two summers with a professor, he did ridiculously higher math, and he made great friends. It was a choice that has given him a richly textured life, and I think he'd say he got joy out of it, too.

After college, he and the girlfriend parted. Although I have no right to feel proud of her I am proud of her dedication to and zeal for her work, and the fact that she steamed straight into adult life with a profession. Her sense of determination and focus all the way along was a force to envy and admire. I've often thought about writing her a letter, telling her that, and also, thanking her. First, she put up with our snobbery and our tedium with grace. Second, she helped my son come to his college decision without self-interest. Third, she was able to make him do all the things I'd nagged him to do for years. He wrote thank-you notes, he cleaned up after himself, he emptied the dishwasher, he expressed gratitude. Fourth, she taught him her own foolproof brand of organization, which

involved color-coded Post-its and ticklers. Fifth, she reintro-
duced him to the world outside of cyberspace. She was pure
gold, that girl. She civilized him as perhaps only the female can
do. As a bonus, I'm not sure anyone has ever laughed harder at
his jokes. For six years she loved him and he loved her back,
with all the attendant joys and problems and sorrows, which is
probably the best education you can get.

Hooked

. . . .

Laurie Kutchins

*O*ur son started casting his first fly rod before he was out of a night diaper. Never mind that it was his own creation, a three-foot aspen branch with a long piece of red yarn tied to the end. I took him to his baptismal waters, the Wind River of Wyoming. He stood in the shallow cusp of continental snowmelt, untethered river flowing east of the Divide; he cast and kept casting, longer than most toddlers would. When no fish appeared at the end of his yarn he decided the trout were napping and he'd try again later.

"Later" became high school, and all the persistence of that small boy casting into the headwaters was his to harvest toward college. High school seniors are explicitly coached to stand out, when what my son had really excelled at was silence and camouflage. As a young but skilled fly-fisherman, he understood best how *not* to be seen or heard by the wary trout that hid themselves among the rocks and riffles.

In college admissions vernacular, an applicant is "hooked" if he or she is an obvious shoo-in: a case of legacy or development, a category underrepresented, a competitive athlete. Beyond admissions lingo for "hooked" swarms the vast sea of "hopefuls."

The majority of college applicants. They are expected to find an angle, to assert uniqueness and vision out of something they are hardly wired to see yet—the trajectory, cohesion, and purpose of their lives. As I watched my son wrangle with the application essays—those dauntingly small boxes on the forms, small and tedious like his flies hung up in the leafy brush of the riverbank—I came to realize that a seventeen-year-old brain is not made to fathom its full potential, its straw-to-become-gold, its future contributions, let alone articulate them in a succinct 250- to 500-word essay. Yet crank them out they must.

In our son's life, fly-fishing to excess was his version of normal; he tied PMDs and wooly buggers in our den on weekends when other teens were out carousing. "The difference between us, Dad," he announced back in eighth grade, "is that you love to fly-fish, but I *live* to fly-fish!" That was the developmental phase, when he aspired to be a trout bum and began to see himself at Montana State in Bozeman, the school closest to his favorite rivers.

"Son, you don't pick a college for its nearby waters." Thus our counsel began. He kept tying flies, studying streams, fishing his way through high school. He joined Trout Unlimited, made the U.S. Youth Fly Fishing Team. Classmates sometimes teased him about fishing being his only team sport, and joked about the hand-tied flies hooked in his sweat-stained cap. Out of the four directions the friendly first mailings from colleges and universities began to trickle in.

· · · · · · · ·

THIS MORNING, TWO days after moving him into a dorm, his room at home has the feel of detritus, the guts-and-bones bucket on a dock. When I walk into it, I am met by the smells and clutter that remain after a boy's last year at home: his high school letter, ring, diploma, yearbooks, old note-books, dirty socks, thrift store suits with vests, abandoned fly rods, lines, elk hair caddis, and feathery nymphs flung across dresser and desk. I find his copy of *Trout Bum* by John Gier-ach fallen between his mattress and headboard.

I lift his windows wide to air the room out. The August breeze stirs up the papers still in piles on his floor from all last year. A page of the Common App comes floating up, a sample he later perfected after countless drafts. I flip another page over and smile to find his earliest awkward, insufficient at-tempt at The Essay. Evidence he was casting about for an obvious, ambitious risk, it began, *What I remember most viv-idly were the boobs*. . . . and went on to describe the time he took Dress-Up Day literally in third grade. All trash and scratch paper now.

Just a year ago he began the process daunted, overwhelmed, disorganized, unprepared, unfocused. He completed it two days ago on Move-in Day, a Jefferson Scholar at the University of Virginia, poised, excited, confident, almost giddy with get-there-get-started energy. What brought about such a palpable transformation in less than a year of his life? Amid the grunt and strain of junior-senior years, amid all the questions about what loomed beyond high school, it now seems like some wand was imperceptibly waving over him, getting him, getting us his parents, ready for this graceful launch. Our only job now is to let go, to clean up his room in the wake of his departure.

As it escalated, his college application process reminded me of the egg-drop assignment in sixth grade. He had to design a device that would keep one egg from breaking when dropped from the school's roof. This assignment did not engage our son until he designed, tested, and perfected an invention that held a dozen eggs. He practiced hurling them out our attic window while I scurried to and from the store buying more eggs. By senior year the eggs were colleges he knew little about, and as deadlines loomed, what seemed to interest him was the challenge of landing acceptances into as many as possible. While we advised him to prioritize and narrow down, he expanded and set his intentions on more than a baker's dozen.

Of the fourteen schools he wanted to apply to, he'd set foot on campus at only three. He decided he didn't want to make any more visits unless he was accepted. "I don't want to fall in love only to get rejected," he told us. He knew the stats and odds, and recited them often. It was an unprecedented year for both admissions and applicants, the most competitive and financially ravaged on record. His lists included Ivies and schools more welcoming, in state and out, private and public, small and large, liberal arts and science. While his ambitious, competitive side was driven by the poor odds, his actual engagement getting started on the applications was sluggish at best. His biggest drawbacks seemed to be lack of time management and focus.

In late October I sought advice from his school guidance counselor. Her office had shelves featuring decorative jars of various shapes and sizes, filled with beach sand from all over the world. I felt like my son was one of those sand grains in the roll of the incoming college tidal wave.

"Is he aiming too high?" I asked Ms. Linden.

"Not if he can bring his SAT scores up later this month." One more pressure to add to the list.

"What about the essay? He's brainstormed a bunch of ideas but can't get beyond ideas. He acts like a deer paralyzed by the headlights of an oncoming car—I think he's so overwhelmed he's shutting down."

She nodded. She guided us both through the wave. She encouraged active parental involvement, especially around the issue of time management. Creating deadlines before *the* deadlines would help, she said. We made a big calendar built of safety-net deadlines. With the encouragement from Guidance, we now comfortably accepted our parental roles as Application Coaches and Deadline Enforcement Officers. As November fell away alongside Virginia's foliage and we saw that he was still mired in rough drafts, we made him forgo the national high school journalism conference in St. Louis. "Sorry pal. Been there, done that," his dad said bluntly. "This weekend is about your *next* four years, not your past four." And when in December there was still a daunting constellation of deceptively simple, short essays to write—responses he thought he could dash off in an hour—I resorted to confiscating his cell phone and Internet access for whole evenings at a time. As my last resort, I even took away his vice. Literally, his fly-tying vise.

Ms. Linden read his hilarious but suffering essay about the third-grade boobs, high heels, and dress, understood his intention to write the travails of being unique, and tactfully turned him toward the freestone streams. "Write from what you know and love," she prompted him. Describe who you are, who you want to become, she pressed him. Write about the fly-fishing team, your work with Trout Unlimited. Those feathered, elk hair flies in your cap.

> *I stood knee-deep in the headwaters of the Frying Pan River as the icy water rushed around my calves. Surrounded by five younger teenage boys, we hunched over the seine net we used to sample the stream bottom, and examined our catch of aquatic macro-invertebrates. . . .*
>
> *This is not going to be another typical glowing essay about how my volunteer work at the Blessed Sacrament Church soup kitchen has benefited the poor and taught me compassion. In total, brutal honesty, I despise Soup Kitchen and I dread the Wednesday afternoons I serve pork-n-beans, hot dogs, and expired baked goods to my community's less fortunate. But something keeps me going back. . . .*

How to write a good first sentence that hooks and brightens some anonymous admissions reader; how to sustain it and weave in a legitimate juicy slice of your life; which of your life-risks or fantasies to share, and which to leave unmentioned; how to do all this within the confines of a word count, and under the yea-or-nay judgment of a mysterious power reader. These are the challenges of the college application, challenges that kept our son returning to the computer while his waders hung dry on a hook in our mudroom. The more we suggested that each essay was still in draft stage, the more he acquiesced and got into it. Slowly he started revising, and eventually he was writing without our prodding and nagging. And the more he wrote, pondered, and shaped, the more we began to hear his voice, his essence, coming through.

I believe fly-fishermen must be the stewards of the environment because of our recreational investment in it. . . . If I can help to change someone's appreciation for the environment by showing them its beauty, complexity, and fragility, we might then collaborate to tackle much larger issues. . . .

Expecting to find people grateful for a free hot meal, instead I was shocked when I discovered greed, ingratitude, and entitlement among some of the soup kitchen regulars. Weekly I witness Esther waddle out the church doors lugging two grocery bags brimming with leftover food. . . .

As we listened to him read every draft aloud, it dawned on us that the same focus and tenacity he brought to fly-fishing were now being applied to getting into college. We startled, ruminated, laughed aloud, even teared up at times to be his practice audience, to bear witness. For the first time I think he experienced writing as a mysterious process of discovery. He was challenged and humbled to accept the mess of his own words on the page, and to forge out of that mess a commanding presence, a voice of clarity, integrity, and passion.

As a salmonfly nymph undergoes an emergence into a mature adult, in teaching these kids to fly-fish, I influence their own emergence. . . . I hope to develop a program that improves soup kitchen nutrition by supplementing meals with produce from excess yields from local farms. . . .

It is a powerful and indelible moment when parents catch a first glimpse of mature adulthood emerging in their teenage kid. As his essays took their shape and integrity from his lived experience, and as he found his voice and a way to describe himself on the page, I sometimes stood back from being a nagging parent or a writing coach and simply marveled at the character and potential shimmering inside the word limit.

We found ourselves performing a small ritual when he was finally ready to release the applications to their designated admissions offices. For each school, he picked from my stack of Medicine Cards, divinations and totems from the animal world. Elk/Stamina, Bear/Introspection, Bison/Abundance, Butterfly/Transformation, Coyote/Trickster, Mountain Lion/Leadership—some were the same animals he had encountered while fishing western streams. I read of their powers while he clutched the card to his chest, kissed it in some hopeful gesture, and hit the Send command.

Ironically, our son did not take his fly-fishing gear to UVA. The Blue Ridge Mountains form a soft ruffled horizon that he can see when he looks west, but the mountain streams with brook trout and browns are too far to get to without a car. And he's studying harder than he ever has before. He called us after Join-a-Club Saturday, said he'd gone sailing with the Sailing Club and loved it. Maybe for the time being sailing will be water enough for his angling soul.

Our Quixotic Quests for Utopia U

. . . .

Anna Duke Reach

*I*f anyone asked my (then) four-year-old daughter what she wanted to be when she grew up, she'd simply answer, "A horse." If my first child had responded this way, I would have patiently explained the biological reasons that made this option impossible. If my second child had said this, I might have laughed it off with an affected neigh. Since the youngest was my third child in five years, I had only a flicker of energy to ask, "What kind?" She then described the purple horse she would become, with a fuchsia mane, a horse that was a fast runner as well as a high jumper. *"Wow!"* I said, smiling. "Go for it!"

I remembered this conversation fourteen years later as I was driving her hundreds of miles across the country in search of Utopia U. It took me seven years of college searches with my three very different children (I know you know) to learn a basic rule: Virtual reality is just as valid a part of the search process as test scores, grades, and tuition expenses. Over these years, I've come to accept that my parental role is like that of

Sancho Panza to Don Quixote, listening hard and believing the impossible until I share a vision of each child's dream.

It wasn't always so. We began the search with our eldest quite logically, as if we were solving an algorithm. She found colleges to fit her personal numbers (grades, test scores, school size, student-professor ratio desired, number of core credits required, application due dates) while I listed numbers that concerned me (tuition, books, tuition, room/board, tuition, flight home, tuition). Endless hours were spent trying to merge these numbers to determine the magic formula that would equal admission. By spring break, we had narrowed the list to ten colleges in New England, so we carefully planned out our first round of college tours accordingly. The whole family packed into the minivan (dogs included—what *were* we thinking?) and we toured two colleges daily for a week. Our math just didn't work; two colleges a day wasn't twice as nice: It was double the pain with half the results. We soon learned that visits aren't about math at all—they are about story.

My daughter hadn't had any time to talk with students on campus, or hang out at the coffee shop or the dorm to feel the spirit of place. We resolved to make summer visits with fewer family members and more time to breathe.

The challenge of summer visits turned out to be finding enrolled students on campus, as most go home for the long break. Some always managed to turn up, though. When hang-out time was needed, I was not. Like Sancho, I was merely the sidekick—a Knight of Hopeful Countenance awaiting the cell phone call that told me where to meet her when the visits were over. I spent time reading long novels in bookstores.

Only when we were back inside the car with the windows up did I dare to ask about the visit. I disciplined myself to listen, to withhold my opinions, as her answers came slowly with reflection.

She enjoyed hearing adventure tales about how each student found that college, and comparing other schools they'd been interested in. All these stories were responding to an essential underlying question, "Do I fit here?" although the question was never directly asked. She managed to identify her favorite four schools and we returned for overnight visits to each in the fall when more students were on campus to share stories. During one of those overnights, she became certain of her top choice. When she was admitted there in the spring, she accepted immediately. Many of her friends were dashing around in April trying to figure out their favorite school, and I resolved to start the next search even earlier so we'd never be scrambling to make a late-April decision.

My son resisted getting back on the road early. He compared the search to shopping (which he despises), and recalled the ragged race of his sister's spring break trip and refused to repeat it. He targeted just a handful of schools and we made individual visits to each one at different times. Athletic facilities greatly influenced his impression of each school. He tended to spend most of his time interviewing other high school students on the tour. This confused me, as they were visitors like us. He argued that they might be his future classmates, and he thought he learned far more talking to them than reading college brochures or attending college visit sessions in his high school. During the summer of his junior year, he attended a summer program at a college that hadn't been on his list of college considerations. By the end of the program he decided to apply early decision to this college. Like Sancho, my choice was to fall in love with his dream—so I did, enthusiastically. Many of the friends he made during the summer program also enrolled, and this circle of friends made the first days on campus seem like a reunion rather than an introduction. With two children admitted and just one more to go, I considered myself almost finished with this college search process, but if we measured by mileage, I was less than halfway to the finish line. The third search was the hardest of all, but it gave me insight I wish I'd had the first time round.

Our youngest daughter didn't become a horse, but she had potential as a Division I athlete and flirted with recruitment opportunities at several large universities. After several visits, however, she realized that D-I might exclude her from selecting a school of her own choice. Coaches would make their selections based on team openings, and scholarship monies required her to play as a first priority. This promise overwhelmed her, so she bowed out of the process and began the search all over again. She traveled to several large state schools and applied to one early decision, but when she learned that many of her fellow high school class members had applied early as well, she withdrew, as she wanted college to be a different experience from high school. In January, we began the search process over again and we drove many more miles in search of new possibilities. Under intense deadline pressure, she did extensive online research and took many online tours.

We agreed to postpone taking more tours until she applied to these yet-unseen colleges, and then tour them based upon acceptance letters.

To her delight and my dismay, all five universities accepted her, so we made a dash in late April to visit them all. So much for my resolution to never be in this spot! In the middle of this up-to-the-minute marathon, an "aha" moment finally came to me. As we walked across the quad, she stopped to watch a group of college students pushing each other on a rope swing hanging from a mighty oak. It was as if a Fragonard painting came to life, with brochure-perfect sunny weather, sundresses fluttering in the breeze, textbooks tossed on the ground while fun and laughter hung in the air. In her virtual reality, my daughter was on that swing. She could envision the full promise of college; how wonderful life might be away from parents in the company of friends in sundresses with boyfriends at hand, all of whom would welcome her to this Utopia with open arms. In reality, she never spoke with any of these students.

When I dared to mention loans and core credits, she didn't want to hear any of it, since this sound track didn't match the dream. It was farther away and more expensive than we'd planned, but I was now one with Sancho, so I learned to believe in her dream. We visited two other schools that week but no other moments took her breath away.

The night we returned home, in the waning minutes before the May 1 deadline, she dropped her acceptance letter off at the post office confirming that she decided to attend the large university in the land of the swing. She donned a T-shirt proclaiming her choice and went to sleep perchance to dream. My husband and I were exhausted but raised our glasses to toast her decision.

Champagne moments were vastly outnumbered by cups

of coffee during these seven years of college searches, but each quest ended in celebration. Each dream differed, but the quixotic quest helped us to understand each child's expectations more clearly.

This insight makes writing tuition checks more tolerable. Now that the triathlon is over for our trio, I must confess I'm envious of undergraduate days in the groves of academe. If a college would open the gate for me to return, I'd gallop right in.

Part 5

....

From a Father's Perspective

Market Lambs and Chaos Warriors

·······

Dan Laskin

*I*t always starts with fantasy, doesn't it? We have a photo
of Greg at three or four, out in our backyard, butt-naked,
leaping into the air on the lawn by the garden, his haunches
flashing, one leg flexed, the other sprung-back straight, his
arms stretched upward, outward.

There, by the tomatoes, he's taking flight.

That's where the trouble begins, in a vision of paradise.
Look at him. How could I not let the fantasies bloom? Our
firstborn would become a scientist, a poet, an activist with
a sense of humor. He would play the oboe. Breathe into life
that soulful ebbing: the human condition in an eight-bar solo,
rising up out of the orchestra, then melting away. Why not?
Look at his fingers caressing the air.

My wife, Jane, the saner parent, doesn't get carried away
like this. She simply believes in hugs and hard work. Perhaps
it's a gender thing—men easily captivated by unreality. But I'll
also blame my upbringing. My parents, immigrants' children,
traced the all-American arc, defeating the Great Depression

and the fascists, leaving the Bronx for college, leaving college for the suburbs, prospering as the country prospered, embracing an ethos of rational progress, and imbuing their sons with the notion that they could be anything they wanted.

The grandparents escaped oppression and toiled. The parents climbed into the upper-middle class. Our job was to live our dreams.

And Greg's job? Anything was possible, no? Especially with the oboe. Colleges liked the oboe.

I half believed that Greg's entry into college would be simply an extension of that backyard leap. It would come naturally, like well-tended tomatoes. We didn't have to worry. Especially because both of us worked in academia. We were insiders, Jane a professor, me a writer—a writer, moreover, who sometimes drafted admissions literature. So the guidance counselor checklists didn't apply to us. As for application hysteria, we were immune.

• • • • • • •

REALITY PROVED MORE complicated.

Dreamy and disorganized, Greg lost handouts. *We* lost handouts. Test registration deadlines appeared out of nowhere. We scoffed at the idea of an SAT prep course, then wondered whether we'd been overly cavalier. Never mind, it was too late anyway. We "processed" the incoming college junk mail— meaning that we glanced at it, told Greg to read it, let it accumulate on the dining room table, and ultimately moved it up to Greg's room, reminding him to at least look at it and urging him to send in the inquiry cards. Did he? Maybe. I know *we* sent some in. (Later Jane would put all the viewbooks and

brochures into a box, which was a more organized way of ne-
glecting it. The box sat on the floor until well after Greg was
ensconced in college. Finally, for professional reasons I brought
the box to my office, where I proceeded to neglect it for a year
before dumping everything into the recycling bin.)

When a professor at one of the colleges would e-mail Greg
("I see that you marked chemistry as a possible major, and I'd
like to tell you about the opportunities here at . . ."), we nagged
him to reply. "Show interest! It makes a difference if you
show interest. They note it on your file. They write it down."
I told him: "I've seen actual files. They say: *He showed interest.*" Greg murmured, and ignored us. So much for the advantage of being an admissions insider.

It was around this time that Greg coined the term "preemptive lecture" for the panicky tirades in which I would lay
out scenarios of doom well before anything I was imagining
could possibly happen. Yes, yes, I admit it: once again, captivated by unreality. Let me blame the photo of the little leaping god. The side effects of fantasizing may include apocalyptic
visions and ranting.

It was also around this time that I found myself thinking,
wistfully, "Livestock."

Some background here. Throughout Greg's boyhood, I
worried to Jane that he should have a hobby. No, a passion. He
should be collecting geodes or staging puppet operas. Didn't
he love woolly mammoths and giant ground sloths in third
grade? Why hadn't that fascination flowered? Where were
the true-to-scale dioramas? The precociously illustrated re-
ports on the Early Pleistocene? (And the oboe. What about
the oboe, that collegiate can't-miss?)

"Successful people who lead rich lives always had passions as kids," I told Jane.

"*You* didn't have a passion."

"See?"

Greg got good grades, took AP courses, had a nice group of friends, stuck with soccer despite mixed feelings, and played the viola. Yes, the underappreciated, eternally mocked viola, an offbeat choice and thus almost as good as the oboe. Alas, he never practiced enough to conjure up the human condition.

But he did acquire, all by himself, a passion, bona fide and all-consuming. It came out of thin air—that is, nothing in the family history of toiling and immigrating, striving and succeeding, professing and writing, accounted for it, as far as I could tell. It certainly wasn't the passion we would have chosen. Greg loved, lived for, and surrounded himself with books that had titles like *Sea of Swords*, *Skavenslayer*, and *The Chaos Curse*. Ditto with games like Dungeons and Dragons, Magic: The Awakening, and, above all, Warhammer. Look it up online. Greg gave himself, heart and soul, to Warhammer, with its vast armies of miniature plastic figurines, Wood Elves and Lizardmen and High Elves and Warriors of Chaos and Orcs and Goblins and Dark Elves and Beasts of Chaos and Daemons of Chaos—lots of chaos—and its painting kits and prop-strewn tabletop battlefields, and its intricate mythologies and infinitude of rules, all laid out in an endless series of books at twenty-five bucks apiece.

In other words, fantasy.

"He has a passion," said Jane, surveying the elf warriors laying siege to his sock drawer. "Are you happy?"

Meanwhile, living in rural Ohio, we knew plenty of people, including many colleagues, whose kids' dutifully and happily did 4-H. They raised market lambs, dairy cows, and feeder pigs. They mixed feed and mucked stalls. At the county fair, they took ribbons in swine showmanship.

Lambs. Not Lizardmen.

If you raised a lamb, you had to be organized. Responsible. Realistic. Procrastination wasn't an option at feeding time. Chores weren't negotiable. Messes had consequences. You learned to groom and medicate. You had to see things through.

Livestock. Livestock was the answer. If only we had saddled Greg with the manure-scented discipline of livestock, he would have written that thank-you note to the admissions guy from Bowdoin who had visited his high school. Everything would be under control.

Forget the viola. Where we had really missed the boat was livestock.

· · · · · · ·

THANKS TO JANE, we organized two college-tour trips, the Northeastern liberal arts loop and the Midwestern liberal arts loop. She handled most of the travel because she was on sabbatical. I flew out to join them for part of the Northeastern expedition.

Admissions officers say that campus visits are vital because they give your student a feeling for what a school is actually like. That's true. But these trips are also a pleasure because they take you away from the tensions and humdrum of home, into a kind of neutral zone, where you and your kid are on equal footing, both gawking strangers.

The tour trip is simultaneously a vacation and a reality check. Both of you can fantasize: the parents reliving their own college years, realizing they'd love to do it all over again; the kid silently gazing, taking measure in his imagination. These stone towers and quadrangles, these porches and lawns, the seminar tables and snack bars, the tour guide giving you the local lingo: You're finally here in the flesh, and yet, because you're an outsider, because the place exudes a familiarity that's beyond your grasp, because you have that sense of being in transit, your tour group a temporary artificial family, like fellow passengers in an airplane, because the campus map is disorientingly laid out east-west rather than north-south, because the very air tastes different—because of all of this, the place seems shimmeringly unreal.

It's like finally getting to Paris or New York. Your very presence accentuates the sense of the unknown.

And the reality check part? Apparently not everyone who gets into Haverford plays the oboe. Haverford, in fact, was where Greg met a student who, hearing that he played Warhammer, said, "You're my best friend!" And Carleton had its own Science Fiction and Fantasy Association House. Wood Elves welcome.

It was on the tours that I encountered my first Jedi parents. Organized they were. They carried binders. They took notes. They had read the college guides, surfed the Web site, and picked up the most recent issue of the student newspaper. They treated the information sessions like a press conference. ("I've heard that you'll house a boy and girl in the same room if they're both gay and would feel uncomfortable with someone of their own sex. Is that true? And, as a follow-up, does that apply to freshmen too?") They caught every statistic tossed out by the tour guide.

So many statistics. Percentage of students who go abroad. Percentage who get into medical school. Percentage of food dollars spent with local farms. Number of theatrical productions a year. Number of a cappella groups.

The implication seemed to be that, if you had a potent enough database, you could digest it all, generating graphs on every facet of academic and extracurricular life at every school. Then, of course, you'd weight each factor—study abroad outscores local tomatoes but has a lower value than average class size—and could come up with composite scores and objective, definitive numerical comparisons.

Not so different, actually, from a fantasy game, in which an Orc, with a Viciousness Value of 8 but a Gullibility Multiplier of 6, can be defeated by a Wizard endowed with Bold Intellect of 10 and a 5-point Shrewdness Spell.

Greg never paid attention to the statistics. Jane noted them but didn't obsess. The college tours taught me to relax about all the numbers.

· · · · · · · ·

AFTER THE TOURS, the whole process felt more real to me and, at least occasionally, less overwhelming. Did Greg suddenly embrace livestock virtues? Did I cool it with the preemptive lectures? No, and no. But we now had a vision of these colleges, and even though our memories began to blur (was Middlebury the one with the new bio building, or was that Amherst? . . . maybe we should have brought a binder), Greg seemed to be homing in on some preferences.

The final push was not fun. In the admissions game, if you're on the applying side, December is the cruelest month.

Suffice it to say that in the cold black pit of a deadline night, while Mom snuggled in her shawl, sleepily correcting exams, Dad and son bonded (if that's the right word) over the online caprices of the Common App.

"Dad, the screen for Question 3 won't let me finish my paragraph. What do I do?"

What would you do if your market lamb went lame? What would you do if the Orc picked up a Devious Scorpion Sword? And which of those questions is more relevant?

They say the whole college thing is a rite of passage. That's true for the parents as well, another stage in the never-ending process—so simple to grasp, so hard to practice—of learning to accept your children as who they are, and who they are becoming, not the fantasy in your favorite baby picture.

Greg would go on to Carleton, revel with the Wood Elves, suffer through some rough spots, and finally graduate. He had good professors and generous advisors. He made good friends. It's safe to say he could have taken far greater advantage of the opportunities the college offered. Could have done more to live up to my fantasies for him. Maybe his fantasies for himself, too. It's also safe to say that he learned a good deal, some of which he's aware of now. Join the club, son.

As I write, he is living with his girlfriend and looking for a job. Jane and I need to help him find health insurance. We're hopeful about the relationship, alternately anxious and philosophical about the future. There's a whole new set of unknowns to contemplate.

Meanwhile, he sounds okay on the phone. The last time we spoke, he asked us to ship him his viola.

Flowers Will Grow

·······

Sean Callaway

I've had seven careers in my life. One was as an organic gardener and landscaper in Carmel Valley, California. The earth grew on me. I loved working in the ground, cultivating flowers and vegetables, assiduously making mulch, composting everything I could get my hands on to grow great food—the best I've ever tasted—and beautiful flowers.

Eventually, I moved back to New York City, finished art school, and got married; Paul was born, but about four years later Judy and I were divorced. We had joint custody. I became an only parent and an expert child raiser. When I married Beth, Paul was twelve years old.

I've grown progressively stupider in the child raising business as I became the parent of five more children. What has happened over time is not a loss of wit (if I ever had any in the first place), but rather a discovery that child raising was not as much of a sure thing as I thought it was when only Paul was upon the scene.

When Paul was in seventh grade, I was in my forties, out of work, a loser in a corporate power play even though I really knew my stuff and had been doing a good job. It was a big lesson to me. Quality without salesmanship is just another word for oblivion. This is one of the reasons why college admissions offices exist, and why I have a job working with high school students.

Paul took the SAT under the auspices of the Center for Talented Youth. The marks he received on the SAT were phenomenal. Even though I had graduated college at age thirty-two and didn't know anything about college admissions, I knew that with scores like that, my son was vicariously driving the solid gold Cadillac with the big-time college bumper sticker. I knew that much, but also knew I had no money.

I was hustling to make ends meet. At the time, I was a computer and systems expert. I built a six-level nested spreadsheet that returned a numerical value indicating the strength of fit between a post-secondary institution and my son. Amazingly, it worked. The spreadsheet became a way to analyze colleges in light of Paul's needs. It forced us (note: *us*) to research schools in depth and consider what worked for Paul. The spreadsheet became a repository for hundreds of his value judgments. We started with fifty-two schools and wound up ranking his top twenty in a process of elimination. Paul really had to consider his priorities, and I began to learn the business of college admissions.

I became the quarterback for Paul's résumé—the Arnold Schwarzenegger of résumés—with incredible qualifications popping out of every category of academics, sports, community service, and summer programs. Paul did phenomenal things because he had phenomenal opportunities. He was heavily recruited by colleges across the country. Because of the spreadsheet, much of the emotional nonsense attendant on being courted by colleges didn't touch us. Paul took the SAT for the last time in his junior year. He found himself a National Merit Finalist and finalist for appointment as a U.S. Presidential Scholar. I was elated.

With this experience, I was well on my way to becoming an admissions junkie. I was turning into a financial aid maven as well, calling financial aid offices and beating them down until I got to the bottom line of their financial aid packages and the assumptions underlying them. It was easy to beat down the financial aid officers in that long-ago age of admissions and financial aid civility. They were unaccustomed to being run over by a Mack truck. I had beaten down vendors in the systems business. No contest, I was good at this stuff!

Paul went off to visit his colleges. He was given a checklist of what to visit on each campus. He was given lists of questions to ask, and follow-up questions. The amazing thing was that he did everything I asked of him.

Except . . .

Paul refused to let me read his finalist's essay to win the U.S. Presidential Scholarship. Not only that, I think he took a dive on the essay. Later I found out it was sloppily presented and had a crucial misspelling. No accident. Very unlike Paul.

In his admissions journey, it is one of the two things he did of which I am most proud. Paul took his admissions process away from me—not your business, Dad. I think that deep down he valued his experience and freedom to choose, and rightly saw that being a U.S. Presidential Scholar, eating dinner with the president, was not as important as his life being his life, and that his "studenthood" was his, not mine.

The other defining moment was his choice of college. It

had come down to MIT, Northwestern's Integrated Science Program, or Case Western Reserve. He asked me what to do. I told him that he had been working faithfully on this for three years. He knew everything he needed to know. He had done everything I asked of him. He had used his head beautifully. Now it was time to make a decision from the heart. I was going out for a coffee and to read a newspaper. Let me know how it turns out, I told him.

Paul walked small circles in the carpet for an hour or more until he called the wonderful woman who had recruited him (and put up with me) at Case Western and said he was coming. He never looked back. By the time he received his master's at Michigan, he had no debt. He established for his siblings that a New Yorker from the Upper East Side could go to college west of the Hudson, decidedly a minority view in his high school and certainly in our neighborhood. Paul now lives in Chicago. His bride is a delightful person. They own their home. I am a grandfather for the second time. Paul has become so good at renovation that he could make a living as a contractor.

I had won in the admissions game—with a little help from Paul, of course. And I considered myself an expert until my daughter Laurie's turn came. Like Paul, Laurie went to an extremely competitive New York City public high school. Unlike Paul, she crashed and burned. Laurie had no business being in that school because it was a terrible fit for her. We had not been able to afford the tuition at the small Catholic girls' school to which she had been admitted and which she wanted to attend. And, as it turned out, Laurie was fifteen going on twenty.

In tenth grade she dropped out. We homeschooled her.

Mostly she read extensively and wrote some. Trained in re-
viewing theater, dance, and art, she went to theater, dance,
and art performances, and wrote reviews. It was a very trying
time for Beth and me. Our family had to navigate through
some very heavy emotional weather. The week after Laurie
turned seventeen, she took the GED and a month later she was
taking courses in my university as a non-matriculated student.

My daughter, with whom I was at loggerheads, immediately
asked me to quarterback her path to becoming a matriculated
freshman with advanced standing at whatever institution to
which she might later apply. I wasn't any too happy when, one
night that first semester, she came home late with a marriage
proposal in hand from a wealthy Lebanese student. Our
fights were something to behold. It was tough watching my
now seventeen-year-old daughter doing a crash course in
Freshman 101.

But as she was given more space, she became better at directing herself. While non-matriculated at my university, she
managed to become chair of a student government committee at seventeen and an award-winning member of my university's national champion Model UN team at eighteen. The
more her life became her own, the better she seemed to do.
She matriculated at nineteen with thirty-four college credits
at Gustavus Adolphus College in Minnesota. She liked GAC
very much, but when she discovered her major, Gustavus didn't
have it. She is now a senior at Claremont McKenna.

Paul taught me the journey was his, not mine. Laurie taught
me that people need space to grow. I began to get it. I was no
longer driving the solid gold Cadillac with the great bumper
sticker. I was the one running after the car.

Just in time for David, the possessor of the automatic 80 average in high school, and B average in college. David deliberately didn't answer pages of the entrance exam to the specialized NYC public high schools because of his sister's experience. He was willing to take the risk that we might not be able to afford the Catholic high school he wanted to attend. The kid's great-grandfather, grandfather, and granduncle were all professional gamblers of one sort or another. It must be in the DNA. David got an outside scholarship and went to his high school.

In gym class in his junior year, David was kneed in his head. Up until then, no one, including his pediatrician, realized David was epileptic. He started to have seizures. It tended to isolate him from his classmates who either didn't believe he was sick or thought epilepsy was a mental illness. David was able to demonstrate a grand mal seizure in class one day in May of his senior year, leaving faculty and students believers.

What characterizes David is guts. He does not feel sorry for himself. His college essay—which was very beautiful—described a hike he took on his own in the Redwood National Forest near the Oregon border. We had sent him on his own to California the summer after junior year in high school so that he wouldn't limit his opportunities because of epilepsy.

David is now a junior at Brooklyn College, closer to home. He did his first two years at SUNY Geneseo and became passionately involved in equity issues. We wanted him to be in a public college because it is easier to ensure that public institutions follow the letter and spirit of the American Disabilities Act. David is not out of the ADA woods yet. His seizures are mostly under control, but I learned to do CPR in a hurry over spring break one year.

Once upon a time, father of Paul, I thought I could leave bread crumbs as a trail behind myself in the woods. Like Hansel, I thought I could build a path to one-size-fits-all. The crumbs got lost. Who knows? Maybe eaten. After Laurie I was a case manager. After David, I understand less and less, and have to trust more and more. I can't control events.

Deeper into the family, Neil dropped out of high school. He first went to boarding school on a scholarship, but that didn't work. Then he went to an inner-city high school where he was one of two white kids. The racial pressure was intense. He dropped out, and now he has completed homeschooling. Neil writes like an angel, thinks a bit like H. L. Mencken, and may be an actor, but he confronts me daily, and only now is thinking that maybe his father has some redeeming social value. Neil has built a dog-walking business and helps support the family. We are on the edge of learning how to talk with each other. I hope to bring him into my university as a non-matriculated student.

Coming behind him is ever-steady Rose, who has the social intelligence of a fourth at canasta. She is in her last year at De La Salle Academy, a middle school in New York. Her grades are great. She is tough. I cannot imagine what her college process is going to be like, but I suspect that it is going to be filled with angst. I don't look forward to it. She is a victim of Sputnik, the first of my children to be completely of the new admissions age. Back when Sputnik went up, MIT gathered all its students in an auditorium and told them they had to save America. The dawn of the Age of Aquarius was in reality the dawn of the age of academic pressure. My poor daughter comes home from school with one of those wheelie backpacks that makes her look like she is making sales calls. The homework load is incredible.

While Rose is doing her bit to save America, America has reneged on its part of the deal. *The New York Times* estimated that the cost of attendance at Harvard for four years would be $250,000 when Rose enters her senior year in high school. One can only assume that the costs everywhere else are going to be relatively just as forbidding. While Harvard's endowment will mitigate its cost, what will happen to all of the colleges and universities below the radar screen of the guidebooks that list the "best" colleges, those "other" institutions without a big endowment to forgive loans, the institutions in which most higher education in this country occurs? Will my lovely, precious Rose be surplus because there is no room in the inn?

The idealized world of secondary college counseling no longer exists either, except for a relatively few wealthy and upper-middle-class students. Admissions officers, of necessity, live in a world of enrollment management, whether they want to or not, driven by economic reality and society's status anxiety. The gulf between pricing and support for equal access grows almost daily, measured from Paul to Jack Henry.

Jack, my last child, is as uncomplicated as his sister Rose is not. He is on top of his game. He classifies and orders everything in his third-grade world. His kind of intelligence reminds me of Paul. I don't know what to do about Jack Henry. When he gets to college-going age, his father will resemble Methuselah. I hope I am there to help him. The way things are going in admissions, with shrinking financial capacity, intense competition among students to get in, lack of governmental support for access, and societal amnesia about the value of a liberal arts education, Jack is going to need a lot of help.

If I am not here, he will have to rely on his mother, brothers, and sisters to guide him. If there is a patrimony in this family, it is in education, in knowledge of college admissions, in a decent insurance policy, in a little bit of wisdom, and in hope and trust in God that flowers will grow.

The Worst of Times, the Best of Times

The Scholar-Athlete Applies to College

. . . .

David Latt

*W*hen our son was six he told us he was going to play college football and then become an NFL quarterback. Michael added that after he retired he was going into sports medicine.

We didn't doubt those lofty ambitions for a second. From the time he could walk and talk, he watched ESPN and SportsCenter, following baseball, basketball, and football with the dedication of a religious zealot. My wife and I, on the other hand, didn't know a tight end from a small forward.

Our credentials were in different arenas.

I have had a varied career—as a Ph.D. in seventeenth-century English literature, a television producer-writer with one Emmy win and two nominations to my credit, and a food and travel writer. My wife was a performing arts producer in Boston before moving to Hollywood to work as the founding director of the Feature Film Program at the

Sundance Institute. We are well respected and accomplished professionals.

All of which is to say that our son thought we were idiots because we didn't know one sport from another.

We tried to educate ourselves by watching as many baseball, basketball, and football games on TV as we could. We discovered that the daily newspaper had a sports section as well as the national and local news. But as much as we tried, we could never learn enough to redeem ourselves in his eyes.

We were always playing catch-up.

In grammar school and middle school, Michael was true to his word. He was first-string in every sport he played. By the time he entered high school, he was in the starting lineups of both the baseball and football teams. In his junior year he focused on football and for his senior year he was the starting quarterback.

We learned that having a son with athletic talent is great. I happily videotaped all his games, recording his passing, running, and play-making abilities. I proudly showed the highlights from each game to anyone who came to the house. Like the time he threw a fifty-five-yard completed pass that led to a game-winning touchdown. Or when three defenders had their hands on him but he managed to break away when he rolled out to his left and connected with a receiver a dozen yards down the field.

We were incredibly proud of him. He was a proven competitor and a talented athlete. Watching him play football, we'd caught the bug. Besides looking forward to *The Daily Show* and *The Colbert Report*, now *Inside the NFL* was on our list of must-TIVO-TV.

But having a student-athlete isn't all high-fives and victory parties. No matter the sport, it's likely there will be broken bones, fractures, torn ligaments, bruises, contusions. During the twelve years he played sports—soccer, basketball, baseball, and football—we saw our neighborhood orthopedist so frequently, he joked that our son was a renewable resource for his practice. My wife wasn't laughing. Although Michael was never seriously injured, she hated when he was sacked by a three-hundred-pound lineman or blindsided by a defensive end as he tried to get off a pass.

By the time Michael was in high school, he knew his childhood dream of becoming an NFL player wasn't going to happen. Today's professional quarterback has to be taller than six foot two to see over the line. Gone are the days when five-foot-ten Doug Flutie could be the starting quarterback of an NFL team. Our son knew that if he wanted to play college football, he would have to focus on smaller, Division III liberal arts colleges, not on powerhouse Division I schools, like Cal, USC, or Michigan.

We all know the burdens college applications put on both students and parents. The college-bound student has a lot to deal with—maintaining a high grade point average, writing personal essays, and taking preparatory classes to improve SAT and ACT scores. For the parents there are untold hours spent pulling together the application paperwork and keeping track of an endless number of deadlines.

Because our son wanted to play college football, we knew we had double the work.

If a student wants to participate in a college athletic program, there will be added applications to complete. Michael had always planned to apply to large, well-established universities and colleges. But now there would be a second set of applications to an entirely different group of schools, ones appropriate for his athletic possibilities.

Keep in mind too that just as there are academic numbers (GPA, SAT, ACT) for regular applications, to apply for a college athletic program requires that a student-athlete has good stats and an athletic résumé.

College coaches want to see that the student has participated in extracurricular programs. For five years Michael had trained with a nationally known group called Air7 (now renamed FBU or Football University) that instructs quarterbacks and receivers. To be competitive, he went to weekend camps where the players practiced from early in the morning until nightfall. He followed up with a strenuous training program with a private trainer. He was willing to work hard. We wanted to be supportive.

None of this was cheap.

When a high school student gets ready to apply to college, there are dozens of books that catalogue and describe American colleges and universities. The college counseling center has a library full of these catalogues to point the student in the right direction. If your child wants to study dance, French literature, anthropology, or nuclear physics, the guides will help you zero in on the appropriate school.

But what if you have an under-six-feet-tall quarterback with an amazing arm? Or if your son is a three-hundred-pound strong-side tackle? Or your daughter is a demon ice hockey player? Are there catalogues to point you in the right direction?

While a college counselor can help search out the appropriate academic setting for your child, they are clueless when it comes to helping the student-athlete. If our high school's college counselors couldn't help, who would?

Sometimes high school coaches can help, but not in our case.

To say that we were feeling helpless is an exaggeration. So we did the thing most people do when they feel overwhelmed; we Googled.

Searching for "sports college applications," we turned up dozens of companies offering their services. Some sound official like "University Sports Recruiters" and "Athlete Web Services." Others had a homier ring like "Best Foot Forward."

These companies are private-enterprise clearinghouses for the hundreds of colleges and thousands of student-athletes who would never know about each other without their services. They help the student identify colleges with programs appropriate for their skills and ambitions. Conversely they help colleges find players who fit their needs.

The more sophisticated companies help the student create a professional-looking Web site, complete with still photographs, stats, and video clips.

There was help out there for us after all. What a relief. But in our case, a recruiter found us just as we were getting started.

In the summer before his senior year, Michael received a letter from NCSA (National Collegiate Scouting Association), which described itself as "The Premier College Athletic Recruiting Organization for High School Student Athletes and College Coaches." The letter referred to our son as a "talented player" and identified him as a prime prospect for colleges needing a quarterback. We were asked to call in and schedule a phone interview with the coach who was head of recruitment.

Naturally we were excited our son had been singled out. When we received the call, we huddled over the speaker phone, taking in the coach's every word. And he sure talked like a coach. He was direct, even a bit gruff, challenging Michael with questions like, "Son, do you have what it takes to commit to football?"

The call lasted a good forty-five minutes. By the end we were convinced that our son would (1) have his pick of the best colleges and (2) the services of NCSA would cost a bundle.

Before the call I had confided to my wife that while the letter was flattering, I suspected this was a for-money program. Sure enough, that was exactly the case. With the coach on the phone, my wife and I excused ourselves so we could have a money talk out of the earshot of our son.

The guilt many parents feel as they pursue their child's college prospects definitely reared its expensive, ugly head at that moment. We debated whether or not spending a lot of money hiring NCSA really made sense. The discussion got a bit heated, but in the end we decided to bring NCSA on board. The money would be well spent if we could be guided through the unknown territory of college football recruitment.

The first steps were encouraging. NCSA constructed a professional-looking Web site for Michael that listed his stats and featured action photographs of him playing. I sent them all the videotapes I'd made of his games. They put together a highlights reel, which looked good, but Michael didn't think was cool enough, so he recut the footage and added a hip-hop sound track.

As a result he received dozens of letters from coaches who needed a quarterback. NCSA helped him craft the e-mails and letters he sent in response. When he was invited to visit colleges and meet the coach and team, they gave him tips about how to conduct himself and what to expect from the trip.

By December, things were going well. Michael was accepted into his safety schools, the University of Oregon and San Francisco State University. Within the next month, he received responses to all his academic applications and had been accepted by half a dozen first-rate colleges and universities. What a relief.

But the pressure was still on because the coaches hadn't yet made their decisions.

During this time, Michael stayed in touch with the coaches. The teams that were most interested invited him for a weekend visit to stay in the dorms and experience campus life and meet his potential teammates. The coaches reached out to him through e-mails and phone calls to make their case why he should go to their schools. One coach even sent Michael a photograph of the football team with Michael's face Photoshopped onto the head of the quarterback, that's how badly he wanted Michael to play for him in the fall. And yet, no coach made an offer.

My wife and I were nervous wrecks. We wanted this process to be over. While all of Michael's friends had chosen a school, we were still waiting. This felt like brinkmanship. The colleges that had accepted him expected a commitment.

The date to accept one college and reject the others was fast approaching and still the football coaches hadn't decided. This was way too stressful.

And then, within one week, they all responded. Four liberal arts, Division III colleges asked Michael to be their quarterback. We were thrilled. All the hard work had paid off. There wouldn't be any scholarship money because that isn't done in Division III, but they were all great schools and we were prepared to figure it out.

The waiting was over. He had been accepted by schools he liked. Now all we had to do was make a decision.

We offered to sit down at the dining room table and go over his choices. We knew he preferred a large school, but the smaller environment of the Division III liberal arts colleges offered a more personalized experience. We wanted to talk about the pros and cons of each school, considering where they were located, their academic strengths, what he thought about the coach, and so on.

But our son wanted space to figure things out on his own.

Remembering our own undergraduate psychology classes, we understood that it was important for him to "individuate." After all, he was about to start a new life, so it was important that he take responsibility for his own decisions.

Blahblahblah. We wanted to be part of the decision-making process, but he wasn't having any of it. Clearly he had assigned us roles as observers, not participants in his life.

Weeks went by and we were no wiser about which college he would choose. Then one day my wife was walking on the beach with a friend whose two sons were Michael's classmates.

She casually mentioned how happy she was that Michael had decided to go to UC Davis, since one of her sons was also going there.

And what about the four colleges that wanted him to be their quarterback, my wife asked? Oh, her friend confided, he wasn't going to play football anymore. He'd decided that his studies were too important. Football would take up too much time.

Wow!

All those years of single-minded devotion to sports. All those early morning weight room workouts, afternoon-into-early-evening practice sessions, the bumps and bruises, the excitement of game night, the exhilaration of scoring on his amazingly accurate passes . . . all that was over.

And to hear it secondhand . . . After so much time and effort, we felt we deserved to be part of the decision-making process.

And yet, we were enormously proud that he had taken responsibility for a big life decision. He had, in fact, individuated. He proved to us and himself he could face an important transitional moment in his life, look squarely at his prospects, and make a difficult decision with aplomb.

Flash forward six months.

When he started his freshman year we worried, like all parents, whether or not our child would like the school, his roommate, and his classes. But there was also that eight-hundred-pound gorilla in the room: Would he be okay with his decision to stop playing football? Would we get a call late at night and hear our son regret that he hadn't pursued his childhood dream to play college football?

In his first year he took general undergraduate courses in economics, cultural history, political theory, American governmental institutions, and philosophy. We were amazed at the diversity of classes. And it wasn't just that these were required classes. He genuinely liked them.

Those classes opened his eyes to a world he never knew existed. Here was a kid who only thought about sports all through high school and now he was talking about economic policy during the subprime financial collapse.

Wow!

He still loved football. He joined an intramural team and he still watched ESPN and SportsCenter, but he had moved on and we were still playing catch-up with our son and this was a whole new game.

From the Belly
of the Whale

· · · · · · ·

David H. Lynn

*I*t's not particularly dark in here or uncomfortable. Unless you count the tension rising from the fact that my son, Aaron, is signed up to take the SAT for the first time on Saturday and has done nothing to prepare. Nothing. No classes or tutorials or even practice tests. He hasn't cracked the phonebook-sized prep manual I bought him months ago. So when asked to write about the college application process I can truly claim it's from the belly of the whale I speak. Sigh.

In truth, Aaron hasn't begun the college search in any meaningful way. No visits, no correspondence, no browsing online. And the colleges and universities haven't begun to deluge us with glossy brochures, catalogs, and letters because they don't yet know that he exists—he never took the PSAT, so he and the colleges are mutually innocent of each other.

I'd like to say that this is complicated by another fact: that I'm an educator, a professor at a small liberal arts college. So's my wife. But I suspect it's not true—no, I *am* that professor—but I don't think I'm any more or less tense about this issue than any other parent worried about a child's future.

Perhaps I do know a little bit more about such tests as the SAT, enough to believe them stupid, wasteful, manipulatable, and inaccurate. They're certainly less reliable than high school grades in predicting a young person's performance in college. Yet for the foreseeable future they will remain a necessary evil, like sitting through rain and snow to watch my twelve-year-old daughter flail at field hockey balls, and Aaron won't get into the kind of college his mother and I hope for him—and he surely hopes too, at some level—without doing fairly well on them.

· · · · · · ·

LET ME SAY right now that Aaron isn't lazy. Far from it. The immediate problem is that he's feeling overwhelmed. And that leads to a little bit of digression.

Four years ago my family lived in Exeter in the southwest of England while my wife Wendy and I led a study-abroad program. Glorious country, Devon. The local government schools (what we would call public) had no places available for our children. So we enrolled Aaron in the Exeter School, a private and quite wonderful institution, and Lizzie elsewhere. He loved it. They loved him. The end of the year and our journey home should also have been the end of that particular story.

Unfortunately, after the glorious idyll in Exeter, the shortcomings of a small, underfunded, and culturally conservative high school in the wilds of central Ohio were more painfully obvious. Not to mention the science teacher "demonstrating" his equipment by lightly burning crosses into the arms of his students. Aaron survived it all—he's a flexible kid, good student, lots of friends, etc. The real problem for him was sheer boredom. And missing his mates in Exeter.

It wasn't easy, emotionally or logistically, and it wasn't cheap, but we felt something had to be done. After much debate and gnashing of teeth, we sent Aaron back to the Exeter School for his junior year. He lived with good friends of ours, and others looked after him—the whole village did. This too, and again, was a great experience for him, perhaps even more so than the first year with us. (Imagine singing *The Saint Matthew Passion* with three choruses and two orchestras in the Exeter Cathedral.) I could go on, but then this would become something more than a digression.

Aaron returned to America, reluctantly it's true, for his senior year. Even if we could have afforded another year for him in Britain—and were willing to live without our son for his final year of high school—the English curriculum narrows so radically toward the end of secondary school that we believed he'd be better off here. That too is another story.

By then, by now, we have moved to a city suburb so that our daughter, Lizzie, can also have a better school alternative. So Aaron is adjusting to yet another school and curriculum. It's a very good public school, as it happens. And in consultation with the guidance counselor we signed Aaron up for a rich and challenging curriculum including plenty of AP and honors classes. And he's playing soccer. And cello.

What we hadn't fully realized, however, is how all the shifting around from school to school, country to country, has messed with the sequence or foundations of work that these AP and honors courses assume. It's not that he can't do the calculus homework, for example—it just takes him longer because he's having to teach himself a lot of what he'd missed along the way.

No wonder he's feeling overwhelmed.

Any other parents feeling guilty about now?

• • • • • • •

ON TO ANOTHER digression—because my own history would suggest that going to any particular college may not matter all that much.

In an epoch long ago and in a distant land with the exotic name of Michigan, I grew up with pretty good grades and pretty good test scores. (Yes, long ago but even then, SATs). Somehow the notion got put into my noggin that I should go to one of those prestigious Eastern schools. Not that there was much in the way of college counseling in those days, nor that my parents were much involved. Oh, I visited a couple of campuses. Their admissions offices showed scant interest and hardly tried to woo either me or most anyone else. Not back then.

Of course, in the normal course of things I needed to apply to a backup school as well. Everyone had to have a backup. Because so many of my classmates wanted to go to the state university or were using *it* as their backup, I decided not even to apply. Instead, I'd heard something about a liberal arts college, whatever that was, in northern Ohio. Big on music and liberal politics. That would do. And then, last minute, a friend who'd graduated a year or two earlier returned over

Thanksgiving and talked up this other Ohio college, one I hadn't even heard of, but he was there and liked it fine. Okay, why not? One backup was as good as another. I was heading *east*.

You see where this is going. East, not so much. To this day I don't know why. It used to haunt me, the "reason" for rejection. Conspiracy theories—I had plenty. My theory now: It happens. It happened.

Ohio. Middle of *nowhere*. I didn't even lay eyes on the place until the day my mother dropped me off and beat it—she'd had enough of my late-adolescent male surliness.

It turned out, of course, that the small college in Ohio was a fine fit for me after all. Probably better in the long run than the more prestigious and much larger places out East. By this I mean one thing and with all my heart: not that my little school was unique in any way or perfectly suited to me in particular, nor as a matter of reverse snobbery, but simply that a small liberal arts college and curriculum is the best mode of education for just about anyone. The physical locale surely doesn't have to be Ohio, by the way. They grow 'em in Maine and Pennsylvania, Iowa and Oregon and Massachusetts.

Am I biased? Of course I am. Not only did I spend four years there growing slowly less surly and growing up a fair bit too. But ten years later, by chance (and the toughest lesson of all to teach students is the role that chance plays in one's life) the same small college invited me back for one year as a writer in residence. That was twenty-some years ago. . . .

I speak to a fair number of prospective students and their parents. As a matter of fact, I did so yesterday morning. Aaron would have been among them except that I let him off the hook, trying to take some pressure off. (By the way, he's not nearly so surly as his old man in days of yore. Though often enough exasperated with his folks—well, yeah.) He knows my college pretty well in any event. It's several others that I want him to visit.

Because as I tell all these visitors, I never try to "sell" our school. That wouldn't work and it would be a bad idea if it did. What I do try to persuade them, and Aaron, is that, while universities are great, especially for graduate and professional programs, undergraduates will receive a richer experience at a liberal arts school. Although far too many such colleges have disappeared, many strong ones remain. In the end, students should trust their gut response: Where, they should ask themselves, do they imagine spending the next four years of their lives happily? (Or three years if they're my advisees and I persuade them to go abroad as juniors!)

Far too many people in this country, and Great Britain too, as a matter of fact, believe that the role of education is to provide a direct means to a practical end—a secure and well-paying job or profession. This way of thinking strikes me as dead wrong. Education is best—and most practical—when realized as an end itself. A liberal arts education in truth never ends. That's why we call the final ceremony Commencement. We teach students how to write and speak effectively; how to do research on their own; how to make a compelling argument backed up by evidence; and how to learn and train themselves. These very real skills are much sought after in the business community, in law school and medical school, not to mention in graduate programs as well.

I also happen to believe that the liberal arts enrich

students in ways that will nourish them for their rest of their lives, that will compel them to ask questions about how to make their own lives meaningful and satisfying, and then to pursue the answers.

One way or another, Aaron will sit down to take the SAT on Saturday. I honestly have no idea what to expect. But I trust my son a great deal, and I'm pretty confident that, one way or another, he'll ultimately place himself in a position to choose among some good colleges. What matters to me is simply that he choose one that will offer him opportunities to become a more mature version of the person he already is.

So I guess my stint in the whale's innards will continue for some months yet. Surely there will be both light and relief when the beast spits me up on shore. Just about the time I need to begin paying one college's bills or another's. I wouldn't have it any other way.

Where the Chips Fall

....

Scott Sadil

Five years ago my oldest son received word, one after another, that he'd been accepted by all of the colleges to which, under my watchful eye, he'd faithfully applied.

It was a sad time in both our lives.

I suspect, now, that I should have been more honest—with him, with myself. My son had little but his own wits to support such a venture. We were poor—not in any way that we recognized, but simply because we owned no property, no house nor mortgage nor land, no assets of any kind beyond a couple of books I had written about fly-fishing, a sportsman's collection of outdoor equipment, and my relatively new teaching license, acquired after falling, while working as a carpenter, from a two-story building and breaking my back.

Divorce, anyway, had just about cleaned us out.

Yet to my way of thinking, we'd also grown debt free.

For a number of other reasons, all of them equally sublime, I felt lucky—at least until my son announced he needed my help, financially, to go where he wanted to go to college, to schools we'd read about, considered, visited, weighed one against the other, chosen together one by one.

He settled, instead, for the state university and a hodge-
podge of grants and loans and contrivances that, from what I
can tell, ensure him a long future as an indentured servant—
that is, if he ever stops moving from school to school and,
eventually, finishes a degree and discovers what it means to
make a living.

I feel bad about all this. So bad that now, as my second son
descends into the maw of the college application beast, I've
chosen to stay out of his way completely. Instead, I'm offering
nothing more than encouragement, tax records, test and application fees—and a nod toward the wealth of community support available to kids at a public high school keen enough
about college to take advantage of resources few parents have
the time or energy or even know-how to match.

It looks, so far, like one of the smartest parenting decisions
I've made yet.

· · · · · · ·

THE ELKS CALL. My son is supposed to show up at an interview early next week. Then either a dinner or an awards
ceremony or—something I'm expected to attend with him
Thursday evening.

"Is this for Student of the Month?" I ask. "Or some scholarship thing?"

"I'm not sure." My son sinks back into his reading chair.
His eyes return impatiently to the Orson Scott Card novel in
his lap. He wraps his hands around a mug of hot tea.

"It's too early," I offer, "for Student of the Year, isn't it?"

He says he doesn't know. He throws a leg over an arm of
the chair.

"This could have something to do with the National Scholarship Foundation," he adds.

"Why didn't you *ask*?"

"I'm sure I'll find out at the interview."

I let it go. At the counter alongside the kitchen I make a half-hearted attempt to straighten up the college marketing mail that's arrived in stacks since my son put up impressive numbers on the PSAT test, administered school-wide during his sophomore year. That same year, he took his first Advanced Placement exam, scoring a 5, which translates into genuine college credits earned. As a rough figure, you can calculate around a thousand dollars for a single credit at any reputable four-year school. By the end of this, his senior year, my son will have taken eight AP classes. He's scored 4 or better on all of the exams he's taken thus far. He asks for money for a test, I take out my checkbook and ask how much.

Still, it's a work in progress. I look down the hall into his bedroom and I wonder what's worse, the clutter on the counter or the mess on his floor. No, it's not even close: His floor looks like the bottom of a bird cage. How can he keep track of his . . . *stuff*? Does he have a clue when the next deadline arrives?

Deadline? For what? Which one?

Let's see. He runs cross-country, acts in the school play. He's taking eight classes, plus another at the local community college. He volunteers for the LEOs Club, competes in speech and debate. His GPA is immaculate. Teachers love him. He bakes cookies for birthdays of friends.

And that's just what I know about.

I can live with the trashed room. When I have guests over, I close his door.

Of course we can keep working on what constitutes a *cleaned* bathroom.

· · · · · · · ·

STILL, FOR A month or more I keep bringing up the subject of early admissions.

I've got some inside dope. Like my son, I'm at the high school every day. A teacher, I get asked to write letters of recommendation for kids I had the previous year in my honors junior English classes. Deadlines fall as early as November. There's some strategizing in all of this, and I'm not entirely sure my son has a handle on it.

He says he does.

But how can *I* be sure? I ask around—counselors, the career center, Ms. Noteboom in the college prep writing class. I get varied responses. Depends on this, on that. I could look it up, online, but I've got lesson plans to revise, essays to grade—and in the fall the steelhead prove more willing than any other time of year to rise to a swinging fly.

Then again, who's the parent here after all?

I ask my son: first come, first served?

He explains it to me. I'm slow to follow along. Something about early admissions requiring a commitment at the expense of other options. I get *that*, essentially, but certain details escape me.

My son, however, has shifted his tone from one of patient explanation to a more age-appropriate sigh. I recall a story a friend of mine told recently about demanding her daughter ask the new boyfriend to have his blood tested. I decide to let the matter lie.

Still, when I find out that one of my son's classmates has already been accepted into Stanford, I try again.

This time he spells out his understanding of the process so that even I can understand.

"If I commit to a school, and then they don't offer me enough money, *I don't go to college.*"

I note the hint of accusation but try not to take it personally. Whether or not he has his facts entirely straight, it occurs to me, once again, that this is his show.

It's out of my hands.

· · · · · · ·

NEVERTHELESS, LIKE MOST parents I'm tempted, through it all, to offer an opinion now and then on *where* my son chooses to go to school. Surely there's some store of wisdom, gleaned over the years, from which I can impart sage counsel—or at the very least, an enlightened nudge.

Fortunately, I keep most of these opinions to myself. All I have to do is recall how *I* chose the college I attended. Like my son, I was a well-rounded student, at the top of my class, as good in science and math as I was in history, English, the humanities. I liked school. I liked to learn.

At least that's what I remember now. My parents and I performed the usual calculations: cost, curriculum, prestige. Where was I headed in life? What did I want to be? See? Do? My academic success suggested I had plenty going for me. A good education promised the best possible life.

My son understands all of this just as well as I did. Unlike today, however, the college-bound high school senior of my generation generally selected *one* school, applied to it, got in—and that's where he or she went. I'd like to suggest the virtues of this sort of researched, focused approach. Yet I hesitate to carry the argument far. My son knows that I reached a decision on a college and then I made sure I got in. He also knows that I chose that school for a single, simple reason: There was, and still is, a great surf break nearby.

He's making his choice based on something other than that. Mr. Clarkson, the med-bio teacher, has a great school he recommends. As do Ms. Ramsey, Ms. Rafelson, Ms. Noteboom, and countless parents of my son's friends. He's got graduates from the high school he still sees and confers with now and then. Even *I* know sources of viable input besides writers, surfers, fly-fishers, and other ne'er-do-wells.

It's an awfully big decision. I can't imagine how I could possibly think it was mine.

Still: Is this anecdote or advice?

Do I have anything to offer besides a tale of luck based on a bright kid who happens to be my son?

If I have a point it's this: Kids will figure things out if we give them the chance. Giving them the chance means watching them struggle, wallow, muck around, and sometimes fail. The college application essay I wanted my son to write was going to describe the time, soon after his mother announced she could no longer care for him, he moved in with me and ended up in a math class covering material he had never seen. The class took a test the day he arrived; he said it was tough—but he thought he "sort of knew some of the stuff."

Instead he got a zero.

A *zero*. We were both stunned. You would think he'd have

to know *something* about the material, if only because it was, well, *math*. Two weeks later, he did. I received an e-mail from Mr. Cohn, the math teacher, who said my son had shown up with his game face on and proceeded to score 116 out of 120 on the Friday test.

The point of the essay was going to be that when we try something new, something completely different than what we've learned in the past, we can—regardless of how smart we are—end up getting a zero on a test. For many students and many people, the prospect of failure—even temporary failure—keeps us from trying new things, venturing into the unknown. Yet without the capacity to fail, the willingness to place ourselves in a situation where, at first, we know virtually nothing about a subject or skill, we have few genuine opportunities to learn anything other than more about what we already know.

My son had demonstrated the capacity to fail, without being devastated, in the seventh grade. We still laugh about it. A *zero*. And why *should* it have fazed him? He'd never seen the material. He might just as well have been asked to translate a poem written by Tu Fu.

It would have made for a great college application essay.

But my son chose to write, instead, about the time, when sixteen, he reduced his caloric intake to the point that his weight dropped below a hundred pounds.

I haven't seen the finished product. Ms. Noteboom, the writing instructor, says it's pretty good. Not quite there yet, she says—but they're working on it.

I trust they'll get it right.

· · · · · · ·

THE HAPPY ENDING to this cautionary tale arrives *not* when my son chooses a college, *not* when he gets accepted, *not* when he gets a full—or almost full—ride.

No.

Instead, the moment comes when I'm sitting in his bedroom, on a stool amidst the layers of clothing, papers, notebooks, running gear, guitars—all the necessary *stuff* of a high school senior's life. I'm looking through last year's tax forms while, beside me, at his computer, my son fills out the CSS Profile, an online financial aid form requested by certain private colleges throughout the country. My son calls for numbers; I find the tax form, the correct line. When he asks about Expected Family Contribution, I struggle with the facts one more time. Sell the canoe? A rod or two?

But when has even a thousand dollars looked so small as to seem the same as nothing at all?

"Zero," I say at last.

"Zero?"

I nod.

My son strikes the keyboard again.

There's a pause, then, a moment as intimate as a father and son can possibly share.

My son speaks up first.

"If they want me, I guess they'll have to pay my way."

Hard to imagine how each of us, he and I, could do much better than that.

Part 6

. . . .

Road Trippin'

The Most Difficult Year to Get into College in the History of the World

Excerpts from "The Neurotic Parent" Blog

....

The Neurotic Parent

March 25

Spring Break College Tour

NEUROTIC PARENT AND Cerebral Jock son are setting off on a relaxing, stress-free eight-state college tour. NP is looking for an inspiring, life-changing setting where CJ will read great books, conduct fascinating research, and learn to think. CJ is looking for the perfect place to spend four to six years honing his beer pong skills.

March 26

Jesuits Are Nice, and They Know How to Name a College

WE WEREN'T PREPARED to like Georgetown because two years ago, a couple of girls from CJ's school got in trouble there for passing Coffee Nips during the information session. Needless to say, the girls were not admitted to Georgetown. (Luckily the infraction did not affect their chances at other colleges— they now attend Yale and University of Chicago.) However, we were concerned that the Georgetown admissions people would remember the incident, and so we left our Altoids in the car.

But instead of a place full of Mint Nazis, we found Georgetown to be lovely, an oasis of interesting people investigating worldly pursuits (and playing serious basketball) in the middle of the most livable part of our nation's capital.

And it has the best name of any college we have visited:

- *Vanderbilt* sounds too elitist.

- *Duke* should be the name of a Labrador retriever rather than an institution of higher learning.

- *The George Washington University* has a pretentious, annoying "the" in its title. What other college uses a definite article? Just imagine: The Princeton University or The Notre Dame.

- *Colgate*—They've got to be kidding. Is it in an athletic league with Oral B University and Listerine State?

- *Northwestern*—The "North" part has some logic for a college located in the northern city of Chicago. "Western" might have worked in 1867, doesn't quite cut it today.

But Georgetown is a fantastic name. It sounds like Downtown or Motown or Funkytown—a theme park of sorts inspired by our favorite founding father, where you can join the Ultimate Frisbee club or get an internship at the Mongolian embassy. The name looks fabulous on sweatshirts and girls' boxer shorts. (Yes, even though this is a Jesuit school, there is a girls' underwear section in the campus bookstore.)

March 27

Most Obnoxious Question Asked by a Parent at an Information Session

TRANSCRIBED VERBATIM AT NYU:

Parent: "I know you mentioned you had a four-year language requirement, but my son has taken every language AP and also every other AP offered by his school. So, what if he had an opportunity like . . . okay, I'll tell you what the opportunity is . . . to be the head anchor on a local news show, and the entire program revolves around him . . . would that be okay rather than the required four years of a language? And could we list that opportunity as a special award?"

NYU Dean of Admissions: (cutting her off) "Sure. That would be fine."

March 29

What All College Tour Guides Have in Common

1. Advanced skills in walking backwards.

2. Effusive about junior year abroad.

3. Proud to display their student ID cards, which can be swiped everywhere for cash, sports tickets, and food.

4. Fearful of losing above cards.

5. Have all taken a lecture class with one hundred kids, and the amazing professor learned everyone's names!

6. Have eaten less than half the food their parents paid for on their meal plans, but luckily they can donate the balance to charity.

7. Can list six of the a cappella groups on campus, but have to think for a minute before remembering the name of the seventh.

8. Uggs.

9. Dance-a-thon fanatics.

10. Thinking of declaring a major in neuroscience, whatever that is.

March 30

Expert College Critiques

OUR ORIGINAL LIST of colleges to visit was too ambitious. But fortunately a girl in CJ's class is traveling in the opposite direction. This compulsive texter has been providing CJ with instant feedback about every school she visits. Early on he was able to eliminate one school from his list because Compulsive Texter told CJ that the entire student body of the selective liberal arts college was "stupid." Then today, she sent out a missive letting everyone know that all twelve thousand students at one Ivy are "too serious." And she has a zero-tolerance policy when it comes to Hogwarts references. When one of her tour guides compared his prestigious institution to the renowned School of Wizardry *five* times during the tour, it was a deal breaker. It seems that this Hogwarts trend has replaced the excessive mentioning of a cappella groups.

March 31

A Leisurely Sunday: Three Colleges, Seven Hours of Driving, Hundreds of Cows, and a Lot of Snow

AFTER A LOW-KEY weekend in New York that includes spotting NYU flags all over the city (soon they'll be on Bergdorf's and the Statue of Liberty), we decide to make up our hiatus by driving through three states and seeing three colleges in one day.

9:00 A.M.—We rent a silver Subaru Outback at Hertz on E. Ninetieth Street.

10:00 A.M.—First stop is New Haven, where we have breakfast with one of our favorite college students. Other than the windchill factor, everything at Yale lives up to the hype; especially, to CJ's delight, foosball and Ping-Pong in the lounge. (But my omelette was disappointing.)

12:30 P.M.—We participate in a "peek" (or "drive-by," as it is often referred to in college tour vernacular) of the gorgeous Gothic architecture of Trinity College. Unfortunately we do not see much else because we cannot find a place to park.

2:00 P.M.—Tour of Amherst College. Although CJ is fairly certain he wants a school with multiple fraternities, he wants to check out a tiny liberal arts college where he can play Division III soccer. Amherst is supposedly harder to get into than Yale, but because there is no coffee available on campus on Sunday, initially I am not as impressed as I am expected to be. Our tour guide here seems like a normal Ugg-clad, a cappella-ish girl from New Jersey, but as an Amherst student, we know she will win a Nobel, Pulitzer, or first place in *Top Chef.*

3:30 P.M.—Amherst soccer player invites CJ to watch an important March Madness basketball game with the freshmen members of the team.

3:30–5:00 P.M.—After an hour in the bookstores and cafés of Amherst, I decide to retire here and begin looking at real estate. CJ calls every half hour to say the game will end in "ten more minutes."

5:00–9:00 P.M.—An inspiring drive through the Berkshires. CJ and I share some incredible bonding moments and even sing "Up on Cripple Creek" together. Sadly this is short-lived because he manages to get loud, staticky basketball reception. The last hour of our journey our GPS guy loses his mind and sends us onto sixteen back roads instead of taking us on an obvious direct route that we discover later when we look at a map.

We're now in the picturesque town of Hamilton, New York, covered in a blanket of pristine snow. It could be the quintessential Christmas card if it weren't almost April.

April 1

Oops—Jeopardized My Son's Chances at Colgate

TOURED IDYLLIC COLGATE University during a torrential downpour. The hospitable admissions people gave us giant, sturdy umbrellas, as well as fruit and Chipwiches—the only snacks we've been offered at any of our college visits. After the tour, the admissions officer recommended that everyone explore the town of Hamilton, all two blocks of it, before heading onward.

I forgot to turn on my cell phone after the tour. When I finally did, at 12:30 P.M., there were three voice mails plus one on my home phone from the Colgate Inn letting me know that their strictly enforced check-out time was 11:00 A.M. I know it's a weak defense, but at this point in the trip it was difficult to remember whether I had indeed arranged a late check-out, or was still counting on the one from the day before.

We raced back to the hotel and gathered the piles of college brochures that were scattered all over the room. (We had not had time to unpack anything else.) The people at the front desk seemed to forgive us, but when we got in the car, CJ reminded me that our tour guide had mentioned that the inn was owned by the university. Certainly, in today's competitive environment, colleges probably consider not just GPAs, SATs, and ECs, but also respect for check-out policies. If anyone from the Colgate Inn happens to be reading this, please give us another chance— We'll be out by 10:59 next time—I promise.

April 3

Investment Advice

OUR NORTHWESTERN TOUR guide was a smart and funny senior male with multiple passions, who already had a job lined up at NPR. He planned to work there for a year and then start medical school. How proud his parents must be. I hoped CJ would be inspired to follow in this kid's footsteps, but at this point in our trip, my son was on overload and only noticed that the pathways were lined with flyers promoting "Sex Week."

So rather than go on about Northwestern, I will use this opportunity to provide some stock tips, which you'll find helpful if you're about to spend $250K on your child's future. Those who know me are aware that I have made some regrettable financial mistakes. But I do feel qualified to recom-

mend investing in the following companies, whose presence
was ubiquitous on all the campuses we visited:

1. North Face

2. Sbarro (plus every other kind of fast food you find in
   a suburban food court)

3. Apple

3. Bed, Bath & Beyond (they have the monopoly on the
   model dorm rooms)

4. J. Crew

5. Samsung

6. Chili's

7. Verizon

8. Anheuser-Busch

9. Red Bull

10. Florence Tourist Board (Just about every junior in
    America spends his or her junior year there, and nobody
    leaves without hitting the Prada outlet malls.)

April 16

Vows

MY YOUNGER SON (Brown '16) is just an eighth grader, but
thanks to me, he is already anxious about the college process.

Last night he asked, "Mom, how does a school become prestigious?"

Good question. He sees his older brother getting mail every day from fabulous-sounding colleges that nobody has ever heard of. Some of these fine schools even say they have scholarship money available for CJ, although they found him by purchasing a mailing list.

"Unfortunately," I told Brown, "although there are more than 2,300 colleges in the country, there are only seventeen that people want to attend."

"How does a college get on that list?" he asked. "Strong academics?"

I explained that college prestige does not just come from strong academics; in fact, there are hundreds of schools where you can get a good education. Nor are the *U.S. News & World Report* rankings the real measure of a school's status, although those rankings sure do sell magazines.

Then I told my son the truth: It is "Vows," the *New York Times* Wedding Section, that determines the desirability of a college. Thousands of *Times* readers have graduated from college and gone on to get married. But if you want the *Times* to report your wedding and you haven't attended a school like Wellesley or Williams, good luck. Occasionally a Purdue grad manages to sneak in, but only if he or she is a member of the House of Representatives or the general manager of the American Ballet Theatre.

I have sent *The New York Times* the Neurotic Parent Institute's list of new Vow-worthy universities. But for the time being, most college grads will have to send their wedding announcements to *The Sacramento Bee*.

April 21

North Dakota

MANY ADMISSIONS OFFICERS are not only good speakers, but also quite witty. Several started their information sessions with icebreakers, and some with clever jokes. At GW, the presenter began by telling the group that admissions decisions had been sent out the day before. He was proud to let everyone know that the new class represented forty-eight states—and the admissions committee was still hoping to find students from the remaining two. He paused and then, with perfect timing, revealed that those two states were . . . Connecticut and New Jersey. This got a big laugh, because most of the people sitting in the room were from Connecticut or New Jersey.

So what were the two missing states? When the laughter subsided, the admissions officer revealed the answer: Montana and North Dakota. He told the group that in case any of us were from either of those places, he would love to meet us after the session.

Yes, our whole college journey would be different if we lived in Big Sky Country or the Peace Garden State. So, after much careful thought, we are seriously considering moving to North Dakota. (We actually prefer Montana, but Montana is on its way to becoming the new Colorado, which could end up being problematic admission-wise.)

Ah, how I dream of a new life in North Dakota, a life without college anxiety. As a North Dakota resident, CJ would have lots of choices. But what makes the move even more tempting is that once we sell our Southern California home, the disparity in real estate values would put us in a better position to finance not just undergraduate school, but graduate school, business school, law school, medical school, a year abroad in Prague, and multiple community service summers in Malawi.

And, best of all, CJ will have the perfect topic for his Common App essay: how he had to adjust to a place with tornadoes, blizzards, quail hunting, furry coon hats, and limited sushi. Plus, I've already checked, and the SAT tutors charge less for a whole course of study than our guy does for one lesson.

We have already found a home in West Fargo—seven bedrooms for $129,000, and I'm sure there is some flexibility in the price. Because I doubt we will be getting many visitors, CJ can have a whole room to store college brochures. Would appreciate hearing from readers in West Fargo. Where is the closest Whole Foods? Are there mobile pet groomers? Is there a good Prius mechanic? Just let us know and we are on our way. But, please don't tell anyone else about our strategy. This won't work if North Dakota suddenly becomes the new Illinois, the way WashU has become the new Penn.

April 23

Help Stop Tufts Syndrome

THE WEB SITE www.collegeconfidential.com is no place for neurotic parents. Just about every student who posts on the site has perfect grades, exceptional scores, grew up in an igloo with multigenerational Inuit relatives, and has recently sold a patent to Intel. These superhumans usually want to know their chances at top schools, but occasionally ask others for nurturing and support.

Today I discovered a desperate College Confidential post from a senior, gender unknown, with the screen name of weisenheimer2u. Weisenheimer wanted to know if anyone could figure out why he or she was wait-listed at Bard. There was an immediate response from randomname25, whose theory was that Weisenheimer was the victim of "Tufts syndrome."

Weisenheimer2u:

WAIT-LISTED with 2340 SAT, 3.9 GPA

I just got wait-listed today! I thought I was in for sure and Bard is my #1 school. Does anyone know WHY? I mean I know Bard is a great school but I thought I was qualified:

GPA UW: 3.9

GPA W: 5.2

SAT: 780 CR/800 M/760 W

SAT II: Math level 2 800/French 760/Chemistry 780/ Physics 800

ECs: Captain of the math team, co-captain of Science Olympiad, co-captain of the chess team, volunteer tutor, started own Web design company.

Why on earth did they reject me? I know I must sound stuck up but my stats are above their accepted averages, I'm a good student, and I thought my ECs were good enough. What was missing?

Here is the answer from randomname25:

Tufts Syndrome

What exactly is Tufts Syndrome? According to Wikipedia (yes, I'm aware that you're not supposed to cite Wikipedia as a reference, but I'm not a college student), Tufts Syndrome is a synonym for "Yield Protection." This occurs when a university turns down highly qualified students who seem to be using that university as a safety school. Top colleges such as Tufts reject or wait-list these students in order to keep their admissions yield high. They want to admit students who are really going to attend.

Now, as evidenced by Weisenheimer's post, Tufts Syndrome has spread to Bard. I have also heard that UC Davis and Pitzer have been wait-listing valedictorians and dolphin trainers, assuming they're not really interested and will go to Stanford or Pomona instead.

The Neurotic Parent Institute predicts that Tufts Syndrome will reach epidemic proportions by 2009. It will be impossible to find safeties because if you're an outstanding candidate, colleges won't want you because they think you won't attend. And paradoxically, if you're a nice, normal kid who hasn't written an operetta, they won't want you because they think you actually will attend.

The trick will be to find a college that isn't as sensitive as Tufts. Is there a school out there that doesn't have an ego, that won't have hurt feelings if smart kids turn it down? If so, in just one year, that college can become as selective as Tufts, or at least as Bard, because the Weisenheimers of the world are not getting in anywhere else.

But until that day comes, there is something you can do rather than sitting still, watching Tufts Syndrome spread from one fine school to another. I ask all of you to take a moment to help stop this dreaded pandemic. There is no time to be wasted, and you can make a profound difference in a most simple way: First, find a mediocre student. Then encourage this slacker to apply to Tufts . . . or Bard . . . or UC Davis. Once these institutions are flooded with applications from low-decile kids, their admissions people will begin to appreciate receiving apps from qualified candidates and maybe, together, we can get Weisenheimer2u off that wait list.

April 25

SAT IIIs

I AM SO PROUD to announce that CJ has performed brilliantly on his initial round of standardized testing, the SAT IIIs. These subject tests, offered for the first time by the College Board this year, measure the critical thinking and problem-solving skills that a student will actually need in college.

CJ's scores on the following exams were stellar, and should demonstrate that he has mastered an impressive knowledge base for a high school junior.

APTs (Advanced Prom Transportation)—Students are given the task of reserving an appropriate vehicle to transport twenty-six of their closest friends to the prom and afterparty. Then they must collect seventy-five dollars per passenger, more than it costs to attend the prom itself. (CJ did so well on the APTs that he was able to make a considerable donation to the Tufts Syndrome Foundation.)

FMTs (Facebook Multitasking 2C)—Students are expected to communicate with at least 680 friends in a five-minute period, while simultaneously studying for a Calc AB quiz, watching a Lakers Game, and reading *The Great Gatsby*. (Note: The UCs have announced that they will not accept scores from the lower-level Facebook 1C Exam.)

PBRs (Peer-Based Rationalization)—Students research and present an argument that their interim grades were outstanding compared to those of their high-achieving friends.

Most highly selective colleges recommend taking just three SAT IIIs, but CJ is considering taking the **AGH (Accelerated Guitar Hero)** achievement exam in November, just to show the admissions committees that he is well rounded and truly challenging himself in high school.

April 28

Guatemalan Latrines

ONE OF CJ'S friends, Fanatical Planner, has already written a draft of her Common App essay. Yesterday she sent me a copy and asked me for feedback.

FP thought I was qualified to read her essay because I once taught Freshman Composition (as a TA). That was during the last century, I reminded her, when there were completely different rules about comma usage. But she insisted that I read her essay, so I did.

It was brilliant. FP's voice came through loud and clear. Her descriptions were vivid and memorable. By the time I had finished reading, I was almost moved to tears. I waited a minute, composed myself, then called the poor girl and told her to throw the whole thing out and start over. The reason? She had chosen to write about the latrine she built during her community service trip to Quetzaltenango, Guatemala.

Unfortunately for FP (and her parents, who had spent six grand for the experience), several of the admissions officers on our tour had singled out Guatemalan latrines as an essay topic to be avoided at all costs. One university representative said they had received so many Central American latrine stories that he imagined there were now more outhouses than bananas on the isthmus.

So, what *is* a good subject to write about? I did some research and discovered a book called "50 Successful Harvard Essays." A great find because you don't even have to order the paperback; you can read the first composition for free on the Amazon Web site.

And the essay is about . . . get this: *fixing a toilet in Costa Rica.* The author, who attended a public school in New Jersey, writes candidly that, on the first day of his summer program in San José, he ate some black beans, then made his way into the ladies' room because he was desperate and couldn't find the men's.

"I sat down and did what generally one does after eating a lot of beans. I finished up (remembering to throw the toilet paper in the wastebasket, as is done in Costa Rica to keep the pipes from clogging) and pulled the gold-plated handle. Nothing happened. Huh, that's funny. Tried again. Nothing. Sh*t."

The author goes on to describe how, thanks to innate plumbing skills he never knew he had, he was eventually able to fix the toilet. And that essay got him into Harvard. True, it's not the most difficult year for college acceptances in the history of the world. But the applicant successfully wrote about sh*t (with an asterisk no less) while thousands of dedicated latrine builders were rejected right and left from lower-tier schools.

What happened? One theory is that too many people read the Harvard essay book, triggering a flood of theses about *baños* in developing countries.

Or maybe merely building a latrine does not make you a compelling applicant, but stopping one up does.

April 30

Let the Anxiety Begin

PARENTS OFTEN ASK when to become angst-ridden about the college process. Most experts agree that the right time is the last Wednesday in April of your child's sophomore year in high school.

Appropriately, the tenth-grade parents in our school are

kicking off their two years of panic with a College Coffee this morning. They will discuss standardized testing, junior year class selection, early action versus early decision, and, of course, college touring. As a service, I thought I'd share my checklist of essential resources.

SAT Tutor—Good ones must be booked by eighth grade. But good luck finding out who the good ones are (Parents don't like to share—fear of competition and fee inflation). Although the super tutors have no qualifications other than being smart kids who performed well on their own SATs, their fees are similar to what you would be charged by a junior partner in a corporate law firm. $150–$550 an hour.

Highlight Reel Producer (for athletes)—Bring this guy a pile of blurry videos and he will edit them to make it look as if your kid has better ball skills than David Beckham. $2,500 for the ones who add "Hey There, You're an All-Star" as the sound track, more for those with better musical taste.

Audition Coach (for actors)—Although we live in Southern California where there are thousands of audition coaches, it is necessary to fly one in from Dallas so your child won't come off as "too Hollywood." (I swear, this is true.) In just three two-hour sessions, this expert Middle American will help your young thespian seem more conservative. She will provide hair and wardrobe advice, as well as a recommendation for a Head Shot Photographer from Oklahoma. Once the Texan receives her kickback, the Oklahoman will make sure your child will look wholesome in his or her photos. Fees are very reasonable—$1,500 for the Audition Coach; $800 for the Head Shot Photographer (plus airfare)—but hire them quickly, before they find out how much everyone else is charging.

Wait-list Specialist—Arguably the most important resource on this list. Call her immediately after your senior is deferred. She will help you bombard each college with heartfelt letters about how that school was your child's absolute first choice. $500 per letter.

Independent College Counselor—Most high schools provide excellent guidance, but many parents like to hire an independent counselor so they won't have to nag their kids about deadlines or make phone calls to get them internships at cancer research facilities. Parents who say they "never even glanced at any of Tyler's eighteen applications" used independent counselors. Book by ninth grade. $1,500–$40,000.

Co-dependent College Counselor—Similar to an independent counselor, but instead of relieving anxiety, creates more. Fees vary.

Of course, tenth-grade parents, you are in the enviable position of having kids who are not applying to college in the most difficult year in the history of the world. So enter your child in a robotics competition, then try to relax. And be grateful that you don't have an eleventh grader.

May 1

Passionistas

YESTERDAY, WHEN I picked up my younger son (Brown '16), he had just come from a meeting with his dean. He is starting high school next year and had to select his ninth-grade electives. He showed me the catalog of courses and said that for a sport, he wanted to try cross-country.

I was horrified. He has always been a baseball player. Why was he suddenly thinking of signing up for something new?

Then he let the other shoe drop. "Mom," he said, "there is so much I want to try. I might want to stop doing graphic arts and take a semester of photography. Then maybe I'll do a year of speech and debate, and a summer program in creative writing. I'm going to run for student council and start a Ping-Pong club. And I want to take music composition, kayak lessons, and maybe even two languages—French and Ancient Greek."

At that point I was too agitated to drive and had to pull over. How dare he become enthusiastic about so many different pursuits! What kind of kid had we raised?

"Stop right there," I said. "You cannot study all those things. How would that look to the admissions committees at the colleges where you're applying in four years? They want to see that you have just one passion, two at the most. Top candidates choose something they love in third grade and stick with it."

"But how am I supposed to have a passion now?" he asked. "I'm only fourteen."

"Most fourteen-year-olds bound for selective schools have already won awards in their field of choice," I explained. "They know it's a terrible idea to have more than a few interests. So give it up."

He looked down. "But how am I going to know if I like something if I don't try it? Can't I be passionate about learning itself?"

Here it was: my worst parenting nightmare coming true. I shook my head and told myself it was all hormones, and he soon would return to baseball. But in my heart I knew he might be on the road to giving in to his temptations. Any day, I imagined, I would be getting a call from the dean of students, letting me know that he was experimenting with both photography and Greek.

This was something that needed to be nipped in the bud. I dropped him off at his Little League practice, and made a note to look into intervention programs.

May 24

Making the Cut: The Right Preschool = The Right College

CJ GRADUATED FROM Blue Dolphin Preschool in 1995. Last night we had a reunion barbeque with five other BD families, all with sons who had been CJ's best friends when they were three, four, and five.

Our get-together was a celebration of the high school graduation of the three older boys, who were born in the summer of 1990. The three younger boys, including CJ, were born in the fall of 1990. They attended Pre-K and started elementary school a year later than their friends because they missed the cutoff for kindergarten—they now have another year of high school to go.

One of the families put together a fabulous video of BD highlights, which we watched twice. Wiping away tears, we saw our wide-eyed sons on a field trip to the fire station and proudly wearing jeweled crowns on their birthdays. Our boys looked so tiny and adorable in this montage that, as one of the moms pointed out, it was almost impossible to believe that the big, hairy men sprawled out on the couch were the same people.

The evening was not just nostalgic, but also provided hope. The graduates' list of collective college acceptances was so impressive that one would never guess that this is the most difficult year to get into college in the history of the world. One boy is headed to Tufts, admitted early decision II. Another will be attending UCLA. And the third has enrolled in Oberlin (after getting into all the schools he applied to, and choosing between Wesleyan, Vassar, Reed, Kenyon, and McGill)—but first he is taking an inspirational gap year—part Kerouac road trip, part Katrina relief.

Was it a coincidence that these kids all did so well? Probably not: The parents of the three graduates insisted that all the kids who attended BD Preschool got into phenomenal colleges.

So what was it about Blue Dolphin that gave our kids such an impressive head start? This was a school that offered very little in the way of traditional academics. There was no counting and I don't even remember the students singing the alphabet. The teachers were not particularly scholarly—one has been recently sighted working as a bagger at a local supermarket. What, then, was BD Preschool's secret?

A preliminary study by the Neurotic Parent Institute has revealed that the curriculum was primarily comprised of the following:

1. Singing

2. Cooking

3. Sand play

4. Guinea pig care

5. Holiday celebrations

Sounds like fun, but certainly these were not the learning endeavors that sent our boys to Tufts, UCLA, and Oberlin.

Then, after more intensive research, we discovered the answer: scissors.

Yes, BD Preschool emphasized cutting skills. So much so that during one of our parent/teacher conferences, CJ's teacher instructed us to start CJ on an intensive practice regime because he wasn't cutting anywhere near the dotted line on his work sheets. At first we contemplated hiring a scissors tutor, but fortunately we had both remembered enough about shears from our own preschool days to help our son on our own.

CJ worked so hard perfecting his scissors skills that by the time he started kindergarten, you never would have guessed that he had overcome such a severe disability.

And I guess that by next year, we will find out if the early cutting instruction paid off.

May 27

Wait List Donor Bank

THE NEUROTIC PARENT recently received this comment from a reader:

I have a niece who got into Middlebury off the wait list and gave up her slot at Hamilton and her brother got into Emerson off the wait list, which opens up a slot at Northeastern. How can we find out who gave them their spots . . . and who received the places they gave up?

This comment reflects a new trend that is unfolding for students who are admitted to their dream colleges from wait lists. Mere acceptance was once cause enough for celebration. But now many wait list recipients feel a need to know the identity of the anonymous donors who made it possible for them to enroll at their reach schools.

With this in mind, the Neurotic Parent Institute has started a new foundation, Wait List Donor Trace. Using cutting-edge research methods, we will locate the girl or boy who gave your child the gift of matriculation. And for a nominal fee, you can receive periodic updates about how your donor is faring at the better school that let him or her in at the last moment.

We are also starting a Wait List Donor Bank. Top students can now be proactive in giving a lucky girl or boy their hand-me-down acceptances.

So, if you are someone like Mr. 2400, CJ's friend who just achieved a perfect score on the SAT, here's a simple strategy that could potentially touch the lives of thousands of students all over the world: Apply to eighteen colleges. You will probably be accepted at sixteen. Send in deposits to every college that accepts you. Then, when you get the call from Harvard or Princeton, you can provide places to sixteen lucky wait list recipients. Not only do you get to go to a prestigious school, but you can also help other human beings in limbo, like the Middlebury and Emerson kids mentioned above.

This act of selflessness will take much less effort than going to Namibia to work with the baboons, and will give you the incomparable satisfaction of having made a difference in the life of an eleventh grader who has had to overcome the misfortune of having been born in 1991.

August 2

A Midsummer's Reality Check

IT'S AUGUST. THIS is the time, according to all the specialists, to get a jump start on all the stressful tasks that define senior year.

After a major research study, the Neurotic Parent Institute has created two different checklists for rising seniors, one for each gender.

August To-do List for Girls:

1. Finalize college list.

2. Download Common App.

3. Complete rough drafts of three short and three long essays.

4. Set up appointment with college counselor for essay feedback.

5. Contact teachers to ask for recommendations.

6. Write thank-you notes to above teachers.

7. Take weekly SAT II practice exams.

8. E-mail college admissions officers with well-researched questions about potential majors.

9. Organize fundraiser to benefit Tanzanian AIDS orphans.

10. Shop for college interview wardrobe.

Most girls we know are well on their way to completing the tasks outlined on the above list, so they will be able to focus on their challenging senior year course loads and SAT retakes.

Here is the August To-do List for Boys, which demands as much as they can reasonably handle:

1. Turn on computer.

2. Download Common App.

3. Take a break and go to the beach—Why stress now? That's what December is for.

September 28

Senior Year Separation Anxiety

EVERYTHING THAT CJ does might be "the last time." Yesterday, my birthday, was the last trip to Bakersfield for soccer. I guess I can live without going there again in ninety-five-degree weather, or in the pouring rain. But once I went off to college, did I ever again see my mother on her birthday?

October 12

The List

CJ HAS CREATED his final college list. He has included three reaches, two matches, four fifty-fifties, and four likelies. His school has discouraged the terms "match" and "safety," but if we could use them, the list would look like this: 1 super-reach; 1 reach; 2 matches; 3 fifty-fifties; 2 likelies; 1 safety; 1 super-safety; 1 unlikely; 1 super-unlikely.

I cannot reveal his list to you; I would have to kill you. But I can say that he ended up showing interest in only five of the twelve schools we visited way back in March when I began this blog. He also added two random colleges at the last minute, colleges that we did not tour, colleges that he had never mentioned before.

And he has violated the Southwest rule, one of the most important considerations in university selection: Southwest Airlines, the flexible, changeable, no-penalty transportation pal of the American college student, does not fly to all the schools he is considering. Maybe I could change that if I add it to my list of worthy investments.

October 31

Prayer for the SAT

HERE IS A powerful, nondenominational prayer for those who wish to do well on the SAT and SAT II exams tomorrow. This can be recited aloud in the car on the way to the exam, or silently between sections.

> On this occasion of my [first, second, third] sitting for the SAT exams, I beseech the Almighty College Board to look over me and protect me from mis-bubbling. Grant me the strength to avoid the Passive Voice in my essay. Give me the focus to remember the properties of an $f(x) = ax^2 + bx + c$ function, as well as the meaning of *paucity*. May I stay awake through the Critical Reading section, even if I get a passage about the process of refining rice husks for Tibetan wax statues. Bless my #2 pencils and protect their points; let me be forever grateful that they are not #1s nor #3s. Save me from realizing at 4:00 A.M. on the morning of the test that I have left my TI-83 calculator in the trunk of a friend's car. O College Board, provide me with the will to resist temptation if my classmates invite me to spend the night before the exam partying in a hot tub, as came to pass in a recent episode of *Gossip Girl*. (Kaplan 119:9, 16)

For those taking the U.S. History SAT II exam, add this silent meditation:

> O College Board, Reward me for staying home on Halloween Eve by allowing me to recall the content of the 10th, 19th, 25th, 22nd, and 18th Amendments. And, because I have been a good customer who has paid to take your mandatory, monopolistic exams over and over

again, may I forever comprehend the significance of the Taft-Hartley Act.

November 6

Xanax, Please

CRUNCH TIME. UNFORTUNATELY, I cannot give an accurate report about anything that is going on, because at this point, everything about the app process has to remain top secret. I will be attending a meeting tomorrow with dozens of other neurotic parents and three reassuring guidance counselors, but unfortunately, I will only be able to discuss the pastry selection.

Meanwhile, while I ponder whether I need to change this to a recipe-sharing blog, if you're the parent of a senior, here is a list of people *not* to talk to between November 1st and March 29th:

Parents of kids who went to college three years ago, when everything was different.

Parents of Intel Award winners, oboe soloists, and any sort of National Semifinalist, especially if their kids are applying to the same schools as your child.

Parents of recruited athletes, whose kids have already decided among three Ivies.

Parents of relaxed, grounded kids who are only applying to two public schools—a match and a safety—and would be thrilled to go to either.

Parents who say that "they all end up in the right place," and go on to tell you how much they themselves hated Princeton.

And, finally:

English teachers who believe your child should not have used any form of the verb "to be" in his/her essays.

November 27

Thanksgiving Message to High School Seniors and Their Parents

IF YOUR GREATEST source of stress is that darn college admissions process, be thankful.

December 12

EDITOR'S NOTE: *In this post, the Neurotic Parent subtly announces that CJ got into his first-choice college, whose name she continues to hide from all her loyal readers.*

Embarrassment of Riches

Shopping List for Lucky ED Applicant:

    2 T-shirts
    1 sweatshirt
    1 mug
    2 car decals

Stay tuned for details on how all this came to pass.

December 13

ED Etiquette

Q: MY SON/DAUGHTER was accepted early at his/her dream school. Should I tell my friends, whose kids might have been deferred or rejected?

A: No. Wait for them to find out through the grapevine, which takes about five minutes these days. But do tell all your relatives, and expect them to ask why you would commit to paying $50,000 tuition a year before hearing from Berkeley.

Q: Theoretically, if you have a satirical blog about the college admissions process and your son or daughter gets accepted early to his absolute dream school, how do you continue to come up with material for the blog?

A: Consider writing about premature separation issues, how to pay for college in this economy, other kids' admissions dramas or senioritis.

Q: Theoretically, if you have a satirical blog about the college admissions process and your son or daughter gets accepted early to his absolute dream school, should you reveal the name of that school to your readers?

A: No. But you should give your readers subtle hints (such as "Southwest flies there" or "they have seven a cappella groups") so they will continue to follow your blog.

March 25

Happy Anniversary to This Blog

IN HONOR OF this blog's anniversary, the Neurotic Parent Institute is proud to announce the result of a preliminary research study: This year, in fact, may *not* have been the most difficult year to get into college in the history of the world.

I hereby present preliminary anecdotal evidence—some of the acceptances received so far by some of CJ's friends, classmates, and teammates who have been mentioned in this blog: Columbia (early decision); Yale (early action); Stanford (early action); Duke (early decision), Wash U, St. Louis; Rice (almost full ride); Michigan; UCSB (volleyball); Dartmouth (crew); Penn (early decision); Middlebury (early decision); Swarthmore (tennis); Wisconsin; Kenyon ($$); Lewis & Clark; Carleton; USC (film); USC (music); NYU (theater); NYU (film); Syracuse (business); Indiana; UCLA; Wesleyan (early decision and "early write"); UCSD; UCSC; Colorado College; U of Colorado; Bucknell ($$); Tulane ($$); Emerson (acting); Barnard; Sarah Lawrence; MIT (early action).

I have heard that only five members of CJ's class have not yet received any acceptances . . . and those are top students who will have an embarrassment of riches to select from. Plus, the above list does not include the decisions of many of the early adverse Ivies. The bottom line: Why were we so neurotic? Everybody is getting in somewhere.

Perhaps it is because we have conveniently experienced an economic meltdown that has helped those willing/able to pay full tuition.

Or perhaps it is because the colleges really want our nice, bright students, even though they have only one summer of genome research.

May 27

Countdown to Commencement

SURVIVED THE SENIOR Breakfast, the Prom Photo Op, and the Pre-K Reunion—and the fiftieth birthday of one of my youngest friends. Now it's the night before graduation . . . and the Neurotic Parent Institute has documented that even the least neurotic parents in the grade have become basket cases.

Some ubiquitous developmental issues:

Spending hours going through photos, posting them on Facebook, e-mailing them back and forth, choking up about not just how cute your grad was . . . but at what a young-looking mom you once were.

Agonizing over whether to give the grad a gift (in addition to the requisite two-thousand-dollar computer . . . and the $250K college education).

Discovering in horror that your prom photos are blurry and you need a new camera.

Doing hours of online research about which camera to get.

Deciding at the last moment to self-publish a book for your grad because you're not the scrapbooking type and you have eighteen years of memorabilia stacked up in large industrial Tupperware containers. So you spend hours selecting precious artworks and research papers to include in a gift from the heart . . . but then you realize that it will be a lot easier to do a photo montage.

Abandoning the montage idea because choosing the music proves to be too much to handle emotionally.

Deciding at the last moment to write a poem for your grad . . . but getting stuck when it comes to the tone: Should it be comedic (for him) or poignant (for you)?

Being interrupted from your poetry writing by a group of eighteen hungry Lakers fans who have stopped by unannounced to watch Game Five.

Realizing suddenly you have nothing to wear, especially nothing that looks good with flats (no heels allowed on the turf).

Accepting that not only has your baby grown up, but that suddenly you are the parent of . . . an adult. . . .

Laundry, Lost Luggage, and *Lord of the Rings*

....

Lisa K. Winkler

I want a school where I can walk and read and not worry about traffic," our eldest son, Jacob, told us. True, when he was nine, a neighbor called, worrying, because Jacob was walking the dog while reading a book. We should have known a big city school wasn't for him. But as he approached the college search process, we felt, like many parents of bright, precocious kids, National Merit semifinalists, that he should look at a couple of urban Ivies.

Of course, these visits proved a waste of time. If nothing else, the college hunt taught us that we should listen to our kids. What makes them happy? Where would they fit in? We went through this with three children, and with each the experience was different. All were rewarding: They got into their first choices; frustrating: It wasn't so easy; and revealing: We learned about each child in ways we never may have otherwise.

The first hurdle: accepting you have a child old enough to

apply to college. Our own college search and decision processes didn't seem so long ago. How did Jacob and all his friends he's known since nursery school suddenly become seventeen? Taking SATs, visiting campuses, and writing essays became the focal point of their discussions.

We were a family used to traveling a lot, and mostly by plane. Skiing in February, island snorkeling or touring Europe in the spring. A car trip through New England to look at colleges? We hadn't been in a car together longer than two hours to visit relatives since they were much younger. We'd toss them a juice box, some cereal, leave at 4 A.M., and drive to Maine. This time, they each had their own music systems and water bottles. But like those long journeys years ago, they each claimed a favorite spot in the minivan and slept through most of the trip. So much for three drivers.

For Nathan, our second son, we had to assure him that yes, we were looking at colleges, but he would get his *own* trip. For our daughter, Lydia, then nine, the trip was even more unusual. Her friends went to Disney World for spring break; she toured college campuses.

Our swing through New England included visiting relatives in Connecticut for lunch and arriving in Boston by dinner. We spent a day sightseeing—the Freedom Trail, the JFK Library—and enjoyed the city. The next day we headed to the famous campuses. And this is where the fun began. We realized quickly what appealed to us didn't necessarily appeal to them. Didn't we raise them to appreciate libraries, architecture, and trees? What they liked: descriptions of the food offerings (Ben & Jerry's faux "reject" flavors at one New England campus), seeing dorm rooms, reading bulletin boards.

The second hurdle: sitting through lengthy information sessions with a bunch of similarly bewildered students and parents and taking the actual tours. Often the tour guide alone would be a reason to return to the car. One: they didn't like her accent. Another didn't shave her armpits. (My sons cared about this? That's important? Hadn't we raised tolerant children?) And so on. They rated the guides' ability to walk backwards; they listened to what they emphasized about a particular school and made quick decisions. I skipped a few of these, opting to take Lydia, our youngest, browsing in the town and for ice cream.

The physical plant also influenced how fast we returned to the car. Lawns, closed for reseeding, didn't seem a reason to reject an otherwise reputable college. Jacob not only wanted to read and walk without traffic; he wanted to be able to read and laze in the grass. Too suburban would be replaced by too remote as a reason to cross the school off the list. Another: too much construction—never mind that most would be completed by the time he'd enroll. The dirty laundry and other odors emanating from a dorm room turned the boys off at another large college. This from boys who'd return clean clothes to the hamper instead of putting them away. This from wrestlers accustomed to rolling around on sticky mats, entangled with other teenage boys, exchanging body fluids. And the list of rejections continued. Too preppy. Too hippy. Too much traffic. But we had a fun vacation, even if they slept through the scenery of the White and Green Mountains.

Later that spring, my husband took Jacob to see the suburban ring of schools surrounding Philadelphia. He could walk without worrying about traffic. The student activities were eclectic. Not too far from home and easily reachable by train. One school became high on the list.

By the fall of his senior year, Jacob completed his essays, took the tests, and scheduled an on-campus interview and an overnight stay with a student host. We sent him by train, with instructions to call when he arrived. He called and nonchalantly told us that he left his luggage on the train because he became engrossed in conversation with another passenger.

"You what? How are you going to go to your interview?"

"I'll borrow clothes. Don't worry."

"Don't worry? You'll borrow clothes?" I sounded idiotic; I was imagining if this had been my daughter it would have been on par with a natural catastrophe.

He slept on the floor. His host, Zach, groggy with sleep, pointed to his closet and said, "Take," and Jacob donned a pair of khakis and a semi-ironed shirt. The interview went well. As he returned to the dorm to change clothes, he overhead someone chant:

One Ring to rule them all, One Ring to find them,
One Ring to bring them all and in the darkness bind them
In the Land of Mordor where the Shadows lie.

Students reciting Tolkien clinched it. He knew this was the school for him and applied early decision.

Nathan remembers that when beginning his own college search about a year later his father said: "Go where you'll feel most inspired." He knew he wanted a big university that offered engineering: He'd participated in Conqueror of the Hill competitions—sort of roller derby for high school science students—two years in a row, and loved building things. A musician, he plays trumpet, piano, and cello, and wanted a school with a music program large enough he wouldn't "automatically be first chair" and where he "heard music playing" as he strolled around campus.

We flew to Chicago to see two big universities. At dinner one night, I had him write on a scrap of paper that he'd "call Mom every week." The thought of him a two-hour plane ride away made me weepy. One tour guide began the tour saying, "Wearing a scarf here helps keep the wind out." I mentally planned my next knitting project.

Both schools made the "I could go here" list. One offered the early action option, so he applied to each; the other, his first choice, early decision. In December, he received bittersweet news: deferred by both. By now, my husband had taken over the process, turning our family room basement into a college application factory. Plan B was now in full force as they prepared applications to ten other schools. As I cleaned up after dinner, I'd hear the crescendos from below. "Where's the essay? Where are your test scores?" Nathan sent supplemental credentials to the schools that had deferred him—an essay on Iran he'd written for an Advanced Placement history class, and a compact disc recording of him playing the three instruments. They'd stuff envelopes, and then wonder if they'd placed the right materials in the right envelope. "We ripped open envelopes again and again to check," my husband recalls. Note: If you're not applying online, an investment in office supplies is required.

We waited for April. He was accepted to half, including his top choices, and selected the one closer to home. Two down, one to go.

· · · · · · ·

LYDIA, A TENNIS player, had her heart set on playing Division III. Having a student athlete was new territory for us. Friends of ours told us about the professional video she'd need to send to schools and about coaches calling to recruit their children. It sounded overwhelming. She'd attended several summer programs that introduced her to coaches from a variety of colleges; they encouraged her to apply. For years, she'd been saying she wanted a school where there was decent shopping and eating. Her father, active in his alma mater in a small Midwestern village, yearned to have one of his children attend. The lack of commerce had been a drawback. But as we visited schools, none compared to what this school offered. And the quality of the gym and tennis courts, the status of tennis on campus, and the impressions made by the coaches now surpassed the presence of funky boutiques and coffee shops. In her junior year, she visited, stayed with students, and loved it. She had a video made in August and sent it to the tennis coach, who invited her to return to meet the team after her fall season ended.

Prior to her visit she told us she dreamed that "everyone, including criminals and garbage collectors," was accepted but not her. This nightmare served to solidify her first choice. Yet, en route to the airport, she expressed doubts. "What if I get there and hate it?" Already early November, we'd have to scramble to find other schools. She ruled out her second choice, even though its early action program would allow her to apply early decision elsewhere. Why? Her best friend, Jessica, had her heart set on this school, known for its studio arts, and

Lydia didn't want to obstruct Jessica's chances. Another re-
minder that this decision is in the hands of not necessarily
rational seventeen-year-olds.

She returned ecstatic. She loved the tennis coach and the
team, loved the athletic center, and the overall atmosphere. I
reminded her she still needed to file an application! Being
able to do everything online, we didn't feel as engaged in the
process as we'd been with the boys. She didn't show us her
essays, and procrastinated pushing the button to send the application, making us nervous. She said she felt superstitious
sending it before the November 15 due date.

While counting the days until December 15, our son became engaged. Jacob was living and studying in Israel for
about three years. I felt an immediate urge to see him and
meet my future daughter-in-law, and planned a short visit that
would take me away the day the early decision letter was expected to arrive. My husband stayed back—Lydia wanted him
to put the stickers on the cars—she'd optimistically bought
them on her last visit. She called, elated—the "thumbs-up"
on the large envelope told her the news, and the letter
confirmed—she was in. Informed via a long-distance tele-
phone call, I too was happy, relieved, and a bit wistful. We
were done.

Advice? Let your children follow their passions. Let them
read while walking the dog. Have a Plan B. Allow them to
feel inspired. Knit a scarf and buy Febreze. Enjoy the journey. It goes by fast.

Sound Tracks

. . . .

Joy Horowitz

First, in my CD player, I slip on Dylan. "Forever Young." We're in my minivan, touring colleges in Northern California and, just as my older son, Trevor, and I are nearing the UC Berkeley campus, I find myself tearing up. Something about this moment and the lyrics, conferring courage and strength and a blessing.

"May you build a ladder to the stars / And climb on every rung / May you stay forever young." I drink it in, this tender snapshot of mother and son journeying together and the song's good wishes for his future—wherever he winds up—and realize it wasn't that long ago that he was in my lap at nursery school, singing "The Wheels on the Bus."

As if on cue, he shoots me a look. Then, he ejects my music and inserts his own: "Bullies of the Block" by Freestyle Fellowship, one of his favorite rap groups. "They're not that militant," he says, trying to mollify me. Like I was born yesterday and can't distinguish between gangsta and mainstream hip-hop. Okay, maybe I can't. But even I know that one of the group's mainstays, called Self Jupiter, née Ornette Glenn, forced these guys to take a four-year hiatus, owing to his incarceration.

Still, I listen: The track is funky enough. The lyrics? Beyond "whicky-whicky wack," I can make out something about filling "your fuckin' cup to the rim."

Uh-huh.

Now, it's my turn to hit the eject button. I slide on Paul Simon's "Mother and Child Reunion," a sort of backhanded way of telling him to behave. And, just to drive him really nuts, I start singing along—"Oh, little darling of mine." It could be worse. He might have to endure my singing along with Aretha: R-E-S-P-E-C-T.

And so it goes, this little pas de deux of ours, the getting-into-college hustle. But in our case, rather than home in on the language of admissions officers—class ranking, grade point averages, and extracurricular activities—my children and I cling to the language of music because, let's face it, we must. The push-pull of leaving home is so emotionally depleting, made even more so by our obsession over where our child will get into college, that songs anchor us to what really matters, namely the love to let go.

Even science says so. Recent research looking inside the teenage brain has shown an adolescent "critical period" for music. I'd like to suggest that the most critical time is precisely when we least think about it—during the college application process. Indeed, the music-memory link occurs in the medial prefrontal cortex, just behind our foreheads. So, the part of the brain that tracks chord and key changes in music is the same place that tracks autobiographical detail. In other words, the reason a song immediately evokes a specific place or feeling is because of the proximity of neural connections that have absolutely nothing to do with SAT vocabulary retrieval.

It is all too easy to get caught up in the madness of separating from our children. And the process of getting into college is a special challenge, one where panic, insecurity, and worry comprise a recipe for disaster. Here, I'm speaking of us parents, not our kids.

Not that there aren't good reasons to agonize. It's scary and it's a lot of work—an undertaking most of us feel woefully unprepared to tackle no matter how many times we endure it. But honestly, there are choices to be made. You can freak out. You can muddle through another fat college guidebook, listing test scores and student-faculty ratios and the latest campus goodies. Or, you can accept that, like so many other rites of passage with your child, this one is simply out of your hands.

And, since we all know that "music has charms to soothe the savage breast," doesn't it make more sense to share a cut from a CD you love with your kid, or vice versa, than to argue over missed college application deadlines? The whole process will be over in a snap, but the memories of how you spend that last year together will linger. The question is: What is the sound track of your time together?

Mine has been different for each of my children. For Trevor, whose college essay detailed the importance of his life as a rap battler, the thumping rhythms of hip-hop punctuated our Big Good-bye. In his dorm room at Harvard, he taped up his newly purchased posters of Hendrix, Bob Marley, and Phish as Michael Jackson's "Thriller" echoed across the dorm hallway. That's when his roommate, Chris, drifted into their common room for the first time, and they immediately bonded over Eminem at ear-splitting volumes.

Gus, on the other hand, preferred the chopped-up rhythms

of jazz. A heart-on-his-sleeve kind of guy, Gus would quote his hero, Louis Armstrong, when I nagged about another fast-approaching application deadline. "Mom," he'd say, just like Satchmo, "I'm too tired to raise an eyelash." All it took, though, was cranking up Al Green's funky "Love and Happiness" or Steve Tyrell's "The Way You Look Tonight" to get back in the groove.

And then, we'd listen together to Pops and Ella crooning "Cheek to Cheek (Heaven)," one of Gus's favorites, possibly because he knew it was the first song my husband had ever given to me (on vinyl) and later became "our" song. On another day, with acceptance letters in hand and after he had chosen UC Davis (a school he left after a single semester, and then happily landed at California State University, Chico, our state's first teachers college), he put on Pops singing "What a Wonderful World": "I hear babies cry . . . I watch them grow / And I think to myself . . . what a wonderful world." Cue the waterworks.

Now, we're about to crank up the whole college application process again for our daughter, Lucy, a high school junior. To be sure, there will be John Mayer's "Daughters" and possibly the sound track to the film *(500) Days of Summer*, including Hall & Oates' bouncy "You Make My Dreams." And, without doubt, we'll be singing the lyrics together to Joni Mitchell's "All I Want" from the *Blue* album: "I am on a lonely road and I am traveling, looking for the key to set me free."

But for now, I understand that music is more than a collection of notes and rhythms. It offers us a chance to peer inside our souls and teaches us what we don't already know about ourselves. I, for one, look forward to the feeling of peace that comes when another member of our family heads off to school—just me and the doggie and my husband, the singer-songwriter I fell in love with back in college—and another one of our birds is out of the nest, ready to fly.

Still, I know the ache I'll feel when Lucy is away, happy at school. I'll listen to the music we've both shared and still love, using it like a transitional device—a blankie to salve my wounds. But mostly, I'll listen because if there's one unexpected part of my kids' going away to school, it is this: A quiet house. No front door being slammed. No footsteps clomping up the stairs. No sounds drifting out of a computer speaker. The sounds of silence: *Hello darkness, my old friend.*

Part 7

....

A User's Guide
for Parents

Love in the Time of College Angst

Nobody teaches life anything.
—Gabriel García Márquez,
Love in the Time of Cholera

· · · · · · ·

S. X. Rosenstock

I. The Best, The Best, The Best

MIDWEST AIRLINES PRIDES itself on its big leather seats throughout every plane and warm chocolate chip cookies dished up to every passenger. About a third of the way into our smooth flight to Kansas City, my high school senior daughter, Giselle, tossed her cookies all over herself, me, and our two beefy seats. Giselle—Gigi—always fair, was now also clammy, weak, upset, and metamorphosing into the fairest of them all: She was the color of the 2009 "This Is It" Michael Jackson. I cleaned her up fast, armed only with two cocktail napkins printed with *The Best Care in the Air*.

I felt like Edison accomplishing the light bulb when I

whispered to her that if she zipped up her hoodie, she could be assured of zero evidence of any stain. Like other moms of teens, from the time my great kid was about twelve on, I developed, under the tutelage of her new taskmaster, oversensitivity, a set of skills I hadn't needed during the earlier years of her glorious life: embarrassment mitigation.

The flight attendant flew over with a barf bag and we were asked if Giselle had the flu. I picked up on the airline's desire to quarantine her in the lavatory. Or the back of the plane. Or some secret hold. Gigi looked terrible. Even so she had the wherewithal to shoot me "the look" with nauseated eyes. "No flu. No fever. No food poisoning. This is just something she gets sometimes," I said. "She'll get it under control." The flight attendant bounced up the aisle, got a large number of napkins from the galley, and fanned them on the tray table in front of Giselle. Thus arranged, they read: *The Best, The Best, The Best.*

Gigi steadied herself by leaning her dreamy dark head against the window and directing her gaze outside it. She'd been exotically pale, too, when she was born, seventeen years before. However each pregnant woman gets through her labor, I laud it as a hell of an accomplishment. It remains the surprise of my life to have been spared the hell. I, a wimp, got the gift of a drug-free, epidural-free labor and delivery. Lamaze, yoga, Negative Capability, dumb luck, and a husband who didn't get to pee or eat or sit down for half a day were enough. I escaped the biblical admonition to bring forth one's child in pain. Take that, Man Upstairs. I was handed a healthy, alert, and serene seven-pound girl covered in the white vernix common to preemies. After eleven hours of mamboing her way down the old canal, she had the smoothness of somebody lifted from the womb via C-section. I told her geisha-pale face, "I not only love you, tiny dancer, I like you. Giselle, you are, at origin, and by very definition, without even trying, infinitely loveable and likeable."

The obsession to be liked constitutes the famous quicksand of adolescence. And it is a task equaling any labor of Hercules to find comfortable friends, sisters and brothers of the soul, in a community full of kids whose affluent parents have condemned them to nonstop exceptionalism. My unexceptional public-college-attending parents worked as an insurance investigator and a public school teacher. I graduated from a public university, UCLA. My spouse's employment necessitates our residence in L.A., and in our posh part of the mad metropolis, exceptional people are—ironically and/or unsurprisingly—uniformly jonesed about certain private colleges. Admission to them has been the hottest topic among pregnant women in this demographic from at least the late 1980s on, more eagerly discussed than designer strollers. A canny preschool admission is thought to lead to the correct private elementary and upper schools from which parents, mostly non–Ivy Leaguers like me, can launch an attack on the Ivy League.

But dancing, dancing, dancing a hell of a lot, as do the gorgeous white apparitions known as Wilis when they dance to death the hordes of preppy boyfriends that betray them in a swell tragic ballet known as *Giselle*, well, dancing is an imperfect Westside exceptionalism: It doesn't do squat to get you into an Ivy-League-or-equivalent college. Gige has a fine mind, nice grades, and a rocking ACT score, but this kid is all about dance. Did the rebel in me tote Giselle to her first dance class at three and follow that with hours in the car schlepping her to technique classes, rehearsals, competitions, and performances just so I could opt out of the Ivy League conversation? It is a darn surprising group of institutions in America that are stellar in college dance. Did I mastermind Gigi's passion for ballet, jazz, and choreography just so that when other Westside parents would proffer "Harvard, Yale, Stanford, Dartmouth," I could parry, "Cal State Long Beach, U of A, Tucson, Utah, Indiana, University of Akron"? Nah. Ballet, like true love, cannot be imposed on a person.

I'd offered toddler Gigi low-key days at home with me and our doggies, punctuated by a modest sampling of Gymboree, crafts, and a sane, less-than-hip preschool. But at three I'd been taken to a combo kiddie dance class that featured fifteen minutes of ballet, fifteen of tap, and fifteen of hula! Man, I loved it and it took! Three-year-old Gigi, of the tiny feet and vast volition, adored her easy early all-ballet class and each of the other two million, eight hundred and ninety-seven thousand hard ones that came after it.

Is dancing so much an example of millennial child over-scheduling or evidence of a rare passion more suited to the prior century when *Giselle* was composed and choreographed? Why does my Gigi dance? Why does Gigi dance so much, so often? It is humbling to know a young person with a sober and profound love. My way out of every parental powwow about power colleges was simply a dividend from Gigi's improbable passion. Wesleyan? No! University of Hartford, SUNY Purchase, of course. And Florida Gainesville. But what could Gigi's incessant dancing mean in the context of the environment from whence she came?

Students who are in college right now own as their child-hood's heritage and burden a specific time, marked with particular resonant images: a stained blue dress; Floridians staring at ballots until their eyes bulge; bodies falling from towers aflame; a naked man at the end of a leash held by a female American soldier; the news that goods and services that cost a dollar in 1986 cost $1.99 now; the Internet, the Internet, the Internet. The kids from my neck of the woods also own a mood, a choler, thrust upon them not just by overscheduling but by the-minds-and-hearts-who-brought-you-today's-epidemic-exceptionalism. As I waded through parenting a child in the snarky-and-swanky swamp of the Westside of Los Angeles in millennial times, a few things evidenced themselves as so true, I can pay homage to the late, great voice of my childhood, Walter Cronkite, and say, for this place, "That's the way it is."

My spouse and I recall being surprised by countless parents our age, plus those a little older or younger. At one time these people protested the Vietnam War, marched for civil, women's, and gay rights. They cherished as personal emblems the works of various writers, filmmakers, and rock artists that remain nonstop pleas for open-mindedness of all kinds, pleas for fair-ness. But these parents seek without shame any and every kind of elite status, achieved with any and every advantage they can contrive, for their infant toddler child prospective under-graduate from the first day of Mommy and Me baby group through college admissions and beyond. Gigi tells me she'd like to dance this unfairness to death.

What do we know of this choler and when did we know it? A friend of mine was present at the now infamous birthday party for four-year-olds, the one where the moon bounce collapsed. When she told me what happened, she grabbed my hands. She kept pulling on them, pulling me toward her as she told me everything. There were many kids inside the moon bounce. It was shaped like a big square castle. The parents were listening to live music and feasting on the offerings from a catered buffet. Suddenly the castle was deflating, folding. No one knew why. It became an enemy of heavy, smothering folds. The children screamed. The big square opening was reduced to a small porthole. Cubist parts of small faces appeared at the hole. The parents rushed the enemy. Cole Porter once penned the words, "Though your face is charming, it's the wrong face." The L.A. parents who arrived first at the hole did not believe themselves related to the pieces of faces, wrong faces, they saw first. They did not reach for those faces or grab those heads or grope for shoulders or hands, anything, to pull a kid out. Any kid. Instead, each cried his own child's name. The faces at the exit were pushed back in with force. Each parent begged for his or her precious darling, and only that precious darling, to come out. To live.

After the ugly tussle among the parents, it was proven that getting any child out was the means to get every darling child out. It came to pass that all the kids were saved. None was harmed though all were terrified. My friend's naïveté, and mine, got crushed. Whatever our Greatest Generation parents bequeathed us, nobility of spirit and giving a rat's ass about the common good, appeared spent, pawned, or broken that day. Hell, common sense was only applied as a last resort. Gigi tells me she'd like to dance this selfishness and short-sightedness to death.

Parents make it explicit on play dates, at campouts, Back to School Nights, parties, field trips, recitals, Visiting Day at the University: The treatment for being a millennial Madoffian child who wants for himself all the substance of the group is more attention, time, indulgence, perks. Back in the day, I chaperoned my daughter's fourth-grade class through the acreage of Knott's Berry Farm so they all could learn about their home state's native tribes as part of their yearlong study of California history. It's a long walk through the park to the Native American area. Huge crowds threatened to divide us up or snatch one of our nine-year-olds away. The teacher was barely visible at the head of our long line. I asked a nearby parent volunteer, a dad, what he thought we should do to make sure we kept track of all the kids. He looked at me like I'd pooped all over Camp Snoopy. "I'm only here for Tiffany," he said.

II. We Are Not What You Think We Are. We Are [Purple and] Golden.

—Mika, "We Are Golden," from the 2009 album
The Boy Who Knew Too Much

DURING THE DAYS of that particular college visit, I wondered about the symbolism of Gigi hurling all over that Midwest plane. It turns out she had a not-uncommon physical tendency that, shortly after this trip, her physician was able to easily identify and treat. Just like that. She is no longer bothered by these episodes. Done. Finito. Kaput. But while we were on the trip, I wasn't at all sure.

Giselle suffered through the rest of the flight. She rode stoically in the taxi to our hotel. She didn't ask to fly home. She apologized when I canceled our various plans for Kansas City barbeque, sightseeing, steaks, and blues. She crawled into bed and looked exquisite even as she blended into the stark sheet. We watched The Artist Formerly Known As Lindsay Lohan in *Herbie Fully Loaded* on TV.

I looked out the window at Country Club Plaza and surrendered every chance of seeing anything of the Missouri city where my father, now gone, was born. Each nightfall, this city, mine, the world, bleeding need, ask more of us than striving for individual opportunity. Striving for one individual's opportunity—your kid's—to be spared cruelty's human face, in its petty and its pandemic modes, is inadequate medicine. Gige suggests I use our L.A. experience to write something about the cause-and-effect relationship between individual awfulness and awful outcomes for all. When life gives you an exalted birth experience and a nice kid besides, it is commensurate to respond, as the years go by, with something better than haphazard gifts to charities or two-bit psychoanalysis or fifth-rate social anthropology. But often I don't.

"Do you think it's just so uncool with, like, our Westside demographic, to even be considering a school in a small town in Kansas, and a public school on top of it, that, even though they have a good dance program, and even though we don't agree with the sucky evaluation of all the snobby kids, well, Gigi, do you think there's something about all of their disapproval of a school like KU that makes, er, you, uh, not feel good about it?"

"You're right, I don't feel good, Mom." She pulled up on

one elbow and talked about how her AP English teacher's Oxford education made him prepare them for all kinds of arguments on all manner of topics in any setting at all. Not just for the AP exam. "If you are asking me to accept the terms of an argument about blaming cities, we can't blame Lawrence. I've never even been there." Her head fell back against the pillow. "It's Los Angeles that makes me sick."

I padded around the room, got changed into sweats, and ordered a room service dinner for me and some saltines, dry toast, and ginger ale for Giselle. She acknowledged she had raging senioritis. She admitted she was scared about how thoroughly her life would change in college. She groused about how she had no interest in, or respect for, the boys at her school. She seemed to fall asleep until the room service items came. She then nibbled a cracker and cracked a dry smile.

In the morning light, we made our way out of the former slave state of Missouri and into the free state of Kansas, land of Dorothy and Toto, Dick and Perry. In homage, I drove a rented Cadillac through and past my father's birthplace. It was his idea of a swell kind of car. And he'd never owned one. Gigi continued to feel wrung out. We motored on.

There are more Big Jays figurines, statues, posters, pot holders, alarm clocks, bottle openers displayed in tiny Lawrence, Kansas, than there have been American children transported by *The Wizard of Oz*. Zillions. He's an imaginary bird, this mascot, an embodiment of Bleeding Kansas and its Jayhawkers, a more pushy and more pleasingly colorful Heckle or Jeckle, sporting red for the politics of Kansas statewide, with blue standing in for the micro-environment of Lawrence and the university. We toured KU with a tour guide who was the less-than-sophisticated farmer's son every Angeleno told us we'd meet at KU. He sported the florid acne that forces every college guide to insist: For heaven's sake, don't judge a whole university by one tour guide. And still thousands of high school seniors do just that.

Gigi the Sick-and-Pale took the world's longest ballet class in one of KU's studios while I sat outside and read Michael Connelly and the student paper. I observed the Jayhawk student body and determined that they were much nicer than kids in L.A. When I watch those gruesome prison exposés on MSNBC, I conclude that their populations are nicer than L.A. people. It's a quirk I've developed. Gigi popped out of one studio and into another. She took a lengthy modern dance class. I thought about how to avoid tornadoes. She emerged with a professor's card and the news that this school would be interested in offering her a dance scholarship.

"Congratulations, Gige."

"Thank you very much, Mom." She stared down at the prof's card in her hand. "This is cool."

I drove the Cadillac down a dark Kansas Turnpike trying to get to the world's worst Ramada Inn, which happens to be located in Topeka. I took a wrong exit and drove into a correctional facility and had to rethink the compliments I'd given those inmates on MSNBC. Jayhawk fans were so into KU that evening I hadn't been able to get a hotel room in Lawrence. Gigi and I huddled together that night. I did not ask her what the college's interest really meant to her. Was this school just the first pancake, one to try and toss out before a bid for the most competitive dance colleges? Onward to Bloomington? We drove a cheerier turnpike in the daytime, checked out KU yet again on our own, stayed to see a fun show that included many kinds of dance and the Jayhawk marching band, and got ourselves back in the sky for more of The Best Care in the Air.

Once home, Gigi declined KU's kind offer and then just declined. Joy over the cure for automatic hurling was stomped to death by senioritis, self-doubt, and sadness. She was blue over the meanness, aggressive self-aggrandizement, and insensitivity she'd met up with in our community and our inability, hers and mine, to combat or correct it. Her best friend, a brilliant transplant from Philly heading back East to Johns Hopkins, was shocked by Westside 'tude too. But instead of dancing it to death as she'd planned, Gigi stood still in the doorway to her room. "I have developed some doubts about ballet's ability to effect serious social change," she said.

Gigi wished to develop an entirely different college list! She popped up with brand-new criteria for colleges. Thank God I'd read a book about launching your kid into college that said quite a large number of prospective college students take a left turn during senior year. I listened, said nothing, and surfed the turn.

Giselle intoned a hymn of praise to the sincerity of the students and profs she'd met at Kansas. She cried out for a college that could combine that sincerity with hip sophistication. Sophistication, to her, meant a big city, not a town like Lawrence or Bloomington. She reiterated her dismissal of the damn fine dance colleges in our own backyard, Irvine and Long Beach, because they were too close to home. But she shocked us, and herself, by asking not to be sent too far from home. She yearned to stay in the Pacific daylight time zone! She didn't want the edge of faraway New York's or Chicago's sophistication, she wanted laid-back, West Coast urban spirit. Gigi wanted a good place to dance but was insisting that the college must be, for her, a wonderful place to simply be. There was some danger she would launch into a mad scene worthy of her namesake from the tragic ballet as she said, "But I guess no college like this exists."

Into this world of hurt walked a figure in stunning white from another classical ballet. The best one. A romantic comedy. It was a sign, a symbol for what to do! It was Aurora, our Pound Puppy bichon frise, named by Gigi for the princess in *Sleeping Beauty*.

"You're going to the Dawgs, Gige," I said, getting the message. And it was true.

There is no better match of sensibility and city than that of my Gigi and her Seattle. Even the pallor works. She will graduate from the University of Washington next year with a high GPA and a double major in dance and something the Huskies have for years called Comparative History of Ideas. When I visit the beautiful campus, I walk Red Square and gaze out at Mount Rainier and think of Theodore Roethke or the lack of wins for the football team or the time Gigi told me, gushing, during freshman year, "Mom, almost all of the people who self-select to come here are constitutionally incapable of playing L.A. power games!"

Our beloved children move through their futures wrapped in the flag of their time, our choices, and something more. After a recent stage performance by my little niece, I chatted up her grandma, who happened to tell me she'd recently seen a woman she'd known fifty years earlier in high school in

New York, and how this woman was still devastated to have been kept out of Nana's sorority. I berate myself on the drive home for having expected my kid's childhood experience to be an exception to human nature. I recognize the hallmarks of my demographic emblazoned on this expectation. That's the way it is. I hurried home. I kissed our sleeping Aurora. She kissed back.

Wait Outside

. . . .

Sarah Kahrl

$\mathcal{W}$hy don't you take a seat right there?" the admissions officer suggested, smiling at me and the lobby chair, one hand on my son Hunter's shoulder as she ushered him into her office. The door closed.

Well, of course I'd be in the waiting room. So why was my heart pounding so fast?

This was the last in a battery of five interviews at Hunter's first college visit, so different from the informal, cheery admissions meetings enjoyed by his sister, who was now in the premed program at a selective liberal arts school. Today's campus had another kind of selectivity—its competitive program for students with special needs—and this program wasn't fooling around. We came armed with a required multifactored psychological assessment, health records, transcripts, test scores, and a mandated schedule of interviews with counselors, coaches, and student housing staff. This was the last stop: a meeting with the special needs program chief. This was the one that mattered.

As Hunter grew up with Asperger's syndrome, I'd spoken with fellow parents and found that our autistic spectrum children, like clouds, often had silver linings. Some were musicians, map readers, incredible artists—talents all complementing the flip side of their deficits in the social and language arenas.

Hunter's silver lining was determination. Often armed with minimal skills or experience, he would simply decide to do something and do it. Hike ninety miles in the mountains at ten thousand feet for ten days. Learn to be a wrestler. Attain perfect attendance in high school. Become an expert on social justice topics like racism, or Communism, or ancient Roman governance. He'd stare at me, expressive brown eyes intense. "Discipline. It's the only way."

Such single-mindedness does not always a successful college interview make. Driving to the visit, I asked Hunter what he planned to talk about. "I'm just so mad about what the Ku Klux Klan did in Georgia," he said. "I think I should talk about what the government plans to do to punish people who break the law. I don't think they should be allowed to live in our country anymore. Or there's the death penalty." I took a deep breath and suggested that maybe he should talk about his personal goals for college.

"Oh." He turned to me, looking puzzled. "Well, okay."

The voice came booming from the other side of the wall, "My first, number one goal is academics. I do not believe it will be acceptable if I have less than a three-point-oh average."

Not so loud, Hunter, not so loud, I thought. Academics. From the first day of kindergarten, that had been a collaborative venture. A team of teachers, speech therapists, and we parents would make a strategy every year, creating Hunter's Individualized Education Program. Hunter had goals in the

Program, too—he just didn't know them at the time, because he wasn't in the room. The expectations for parents, however, were clear.

"Be an advocate for your child. Make sure he gets every single service to which he's entitled. And what happens at home will determine his success. Work with him every day." Those were the expectations, and, if fulfilled, I'd be among the Good Ones—the parents who did the work necessary to coax, sometimes forcibly pull, our nonverbal, nonparticipatory child into the "typical" world. And work I did. There were weekly lists of words learned in context. Behavior modification charts. Medication trials. Books on tape. And homework, homework, homework.

The teachers were appreciative. We became a team, with watchful sidebar comments at the end of the day, on e-mail, in phone calls. And every year, Hunter became more capable, freer of the obstacles that held him back, more "typical." He got that 3.0 in his senior year in a regular classroom, at last free of an aide. But a 3.0 in college? Who was going to drill him to prepare for tests?

"My number two goal is athletics. I am a wrestler and I am in very good shape. I expect to be a varsity wrestler at your college."

Athletics was a saving grace for Hunter, and for us as parents. Our high school was a state wrestling power, and Hunter wanted to be part of it. He showed up at every practice, learned, and made his way onto the varsity team. We reveled in watching our son—who in preschool isolated himself in the far corner of the room—engaging in easy banter with teammates, while in the stands we and their parents shared deprecating masked pride. "You all have done such a good job with your son," the coaches would say.

But this would be different. We met with the college wrestling coach, who sat, solid and intense, opposite my son. His Division III team was very good, and he was curious about this recruit from the renowned Ohio high school. "So what do you do to work out?"

"Well, I do what Coach tells me," Hunter replied. Then he leaned closer. "But I have a special workout I do. It's called the Roman Centurion Workout. I have a set of chain mail, and I like to go running in it. I pretty much run all over town." (It's true, real chain mail, about thirty pounds' worth. It was a Christmas present during his medieval soldier period. Try running in it.)

The coach sat still, then he gave a little snort, stood up, and shook Hunter's hand. I was sitting nearby and opened my mouth. I could explain. The coach gave me a look that said it all: Mothers Don't Talk.

"My number three goal is social. I expect to have many friends, and my roommate will become my best friend. I plan on finding a girlfriend my first month at college."

I heard answering murmurs from the special needs director, and Hunter's sharp reply. The conversation escalated. They were discussing. Now they were arguing. Oh, no.

I thought about the number of times I had stepped in as interpreter. The downside of a determined child is that he believes he is always right, and Asperger's makes it worse, stripping away the social filter that keeps most of us from speaking our minds. In his early years, I was always ready with "What Hunter really means is . . ." that would erase the bad first play date, the consternation on a mother's face, the turned backs of a group of boys. And Hunter had friends now, friends who knew him and appreciated his truthfulness, loyalty, and imagination.

But there was nothing I could do about what was happening in that room right now. We'd arrived at the point where there were no more fixes; no more coaching, no more interpreting. It did not matter if I was one of the Good Ones. Nor should it.

"Why don't you join us?" the special programs chief invited. I sat down next to Hunter, handsome and upright in the letter jacket he insisted on wearing on this warm spring day. "Hunter is such a terrific young man, and I am so very glad we were able to meet him. He's certainly done quite a bit in high school, and I am sure you are very proud of the progress he has made. We had a good time today, didn't we, Hunter?"

I sat still as she continued to extol Hunter's attributes. It was over. This was a prelude to no, from a college whose program was built for someone like my son. All that work. All those years. All his determination. I looked at Hunter. He was nodding, smiling, giving a fist-pump at one of the nicer compliments. He had no idea.

"There are so many educational opportunities and services that are available today." And this was the no, polite and final, saving us the trouble of waiting for the inevitable letter. We stood up for our good-byes and, out of habit, I stopped in the doorway as Hunter walked down the hall.

"Why not?" I asked quietly. "Isn't he the kind of student your program is for?"

The special programs chief turned around, the promotional smile gone. "We don't take autistic kids," she stated flatly. "We don't know what they will do in the dorms."

. . . .

"**I WANT TO** go away to college. I don't care what they said at that other place. I want to go to college, and I want to live in a dorm."

And here we were, in June, looking at a community college's online application. I had the built-in prejudices that came with an Eastern seaboard education, imagining slap-dash commuter classes, uninvolved teachers, no campus.

But this place looked good, better than good. It specialized in training students for careers in the outdoors, always a love of Hunter's. The learning was hands-on. A summer work internship was required. A tutoring program seemed strong and organized. And there were dorms, newly built during Ohio's community college boom. Hunter filled out the application online, we paid the fee with a credit card, and he hit "Submit."

"Congratulations. You have been accepted in the Wildlife Management Program." You're kidding, I thought. He's in? It's that simple?

"I'm going to college! Yes!" Hunter tumbled down the stairs two at a time, jumped in the car, and yelled, "I'm gonna tell my friends." The car lurched to a halt.

"Wait. Mom. What was the name of the college I got into?"

. . . .

A YEAR LATER, Hunter sits in my living room, pecking away at his laptop. "I have to file my internship work journal online tonight. Will you read it?"

I look over his shoulder. Who would have thought he could write like this? He's finished his first year, and with some academic bumps, it's been a reasonably good one. The instructors were knowledgeable, interested, and Hunter worked hard. The leap forward in independence happened, the biggest expectation of all for college. I look at Hunter, who's laughing as he texts a message on his phone. "One of my friends just posted a picture of me on Facebook. See? This is me and my roommate. We used to get into so many arguments, mainly about religion, but we're cool now."

"Your journal looks good, Hunter. You don't need me to look it over."

"Really?"

"Nope. You're fine on your own right now."

Sophie, Real and Imagined

· · · · · · · ·

Ellen Waterston

At the all-girls Episcopal boarding school I attended, the bad, rule-breaking, cool upperclassmen, the ones who snuck into the woods near campus to smoke and drink, the ones who secretly met to have sex with Dartmouth boys when we were bused to Hanover for concerts, had placed bets that I would not be admitted to Harvard and made fun of me for my highbrow ambition. I thrived on the order of boarding school regimen, coming from a household that specialized in creative disorder. Whatever wants or lacks I experienced at home I was relieved of. The order and structure freed me. I became more distinctly who I was. The troublemakers hated my goody-two-shoes guts because I liked school, obeyed rules, got involved, did well. They let me know by putting skulls and crossbones on my mailbox, short-sheeting my dorm bed, and ganging up on me in study hall. They lost the bet. I went to Harvard and rejoiced to be in the company of others like me. My diploma in hand, I traveled, served in the Peace Corps, went on to graduate school, married and moved to the ranching West.

Despite the fact that my children were raised in rural Oregon; that their father became a plague on our lives due to debilitating drug addictions; that, as a single mother, I was operating out of a trauma-view of the world, not out of informed calm with time to be sensitive to the subtle differences in my kids; despite living in a constant state of triage—despite all this I still believed, simply because they were *my* children and I was, after all, the one in the white hat, they would see education as the answer, the order amidst chaos, the way out of the maze. And they would go to college, just as their aunts, uncles, cousins, and grandparents had, just as their father and I had. Especially Sophie, my youngest, the brightest of my bunch.

· · · · · · · ·

THE INCLINATION TO try and write our children's lives is a natural one. The overcaring, overbearing parent generally isn't a bad thing, unless and until a debilitating lack of confidence sets in, whether related to substance abuse or typical teenage angst. When it does, anything a parent says can be construed as a negative judgment, feeding a child's sense of inadequacy. Being ambitious on behalf of one's child is inconsequential—even beneficial—when the child is standing squarely on her own two feet, has enough maturity and self-awareness to say, "Mom, I love you, but back off, that doesn't work for me . . ."

But not when the default position is "I am not enough" and circumstances and choices have fed that belief. Not when a child says: "Can't I have a black eye or chipped tooth without you thinking I fell down drunk? So I'm not interested in college. That doesn't mean I am in need of detox. Can't I just be who I am and still have a place in our house to rest my head? Fuck tough love. Why is your love for me predicated on your idea of what success looks like? What education looks like? Why is everything I do or say filtered through your assumption that I am a druggie, a slacker. Fuck that. Fuck you. Fuck you for writing your unholy memoir about sacred me."

My memoir, *Then There Was No Mountain,* was intended to be least about my daughter's struggle with substance abuse and most about what her struggle revealed about my own emotional and behavioral addictions—guilt, shame, denial, magical thinking—all of which functioned as well as any street drugs: slowing my reaction time, impairing my judgment, distorting my sense of reality. In the book I chose the name Sophie for my daughter, not her real name.

Now, six years after the publication of that memoir, I am seated on my deck overlooking the Deschutes River in Central Oregon helping my young neighbor, whose real name *is* Sophie, go over her college essays. A senior at the local public high school, she is bright and excited about life. Neither of her parents attended college and yet she sees what is possible for herself, is ambitious and unafraid. She works two jobs, attends high school, is up to her eyeballs in after-school activities, including playing violin in the local symphony. I point out grammatical errors or suggest she be less modest about her accomplishments or explore opportunities for metaphor extracted from her own experience. My young neighbor wants what I wanted my daughter to want. The irony is not lost on me. The fictitious name I chose and the magical thinking

I indulged in relative to my daughter come home elegantly and perfectly to roost.

How different my experience with the real Sophie is from my experience with my daughter. I masterminded her college essay. I insisted into it what I wanted her to know about herself, tried to force-feed her confidence in all that she was and was capable of becoming. My imagined Sophie, the one I created, wrote this . . .

My Life in Focus

As my hand gently adjusts the lens, the world moves into focus. My finger depresses the shutter and a feeling of satisfaction inundates me as I watch the sun slowly sink out of the frame of the camera. I got the shot.

Maybe my recent interest in photography stems from my desire to bring my life into focus. There had been things— my father's drugs, my mother's struggles as a single parent, my brother's and sister's methods for dealing with what had hurt them, and my own tries to keep the truth about certain events in my life out of focus.

What I realized is it's not possible to keep certain things out of focus without everything else getting out of focus. By avoiding the negative things about my family, I lost myself, my sense of direction, and my family.

I temporarily lost the picture of my childhood that I cherish, the experience of growing up on a ranch and developing a relationship with animals. My mother's worries about money and the personal challenges of raising a family left me and my brother and sister to pretty much raise ourselves.

I didn't value my promise as a student who completed a yearlong research project as a high school freshman on the effect of lawn fertilizer on an urban marshland. I didn't focus on my achievements as an athlete who played varsity soccer as a freshman, who qualified for Nordic Junior Nationals in freestyle and classic competition, who was recruited as a competitive swimmer, who is an accomplished Western and English horsewoman, hiker, and snowboarder and certified in outdoor leadership and wilderness skills. And since there is no letter awarded for many of the "sports" I engaged in—wrestling calves at a branding, moving cattle on horseback, driving swathers and tractors, irrigating acres of land—I felt they didn't count.

I didn't see clearly my abilities as a pianist selected to play at three State Honors Piano recitals, the State Syllabus competition and Bach festival; or as an artist whose mask was selected for the PTA exhibit at the Oregon state capital. My pottery and sculpture won overall in the regional art competition my senior year in high school. My watercolor of a geisha was auctioned locally in support of a local family resource center for two hundred dollars. I neglected to see the accomplishment of my collection of poems and photographs that now grow only with my ability to keep things in focus.

In the past, I failed to focus on what those attributes said about me. I also chose not to appreciate the honor and recognition bestowed on me by adults and my peers when chosen as a representative in the National Helpers Program, a peer counseling workshop; or my selection as a legislative page in the Oregon House of Representatives.

Why was so much out of focus? Because I was not willing to see that I had a personal fight to fight against my drug use during my sophomore year. It blurred my view of my self and my life. I could only see being forced to participate in a wilderness therapy program, and then being sent to Montana for a year of high school. But it was there I found a family and a ranch and a rural community that brought me and my life back into focus.

And now as I begin to see myself clearly, I ask you to do the same. My academic record may not, at first glance, look flowery and accomplished, but look again. Despite the turmoil of my sophomore year, I am a solid student. My athletic skills may not seem varsity quality, but look again at the variety of athletic skills. My community service record may not seem impressive, but look again and you will see someone who met high school requirements while working thirty hours a week. I know what it is to work, to study, to give, to love, to hurt.

I have the camera in my hands, and I bring the world into focus. My finger depresses the shutter. A feeling of satisfaction washes over me as I watch the young woman move out of the frame and on into her day, her future. I got the shot.

Sophie imagined, Sophie real. My daughter, my so-called "Sophie," did go to college for a while and then decided to pursue education her way—holding various jobs, traveling and learning a second language in the process. She is now the student of a life that unfolds sometimes serendipitously, sometimes harshly, always organically, in which decisions are often made because they aren't, a graduate of the school of *pura vida*, go with the flow, it is what it is, whatever.

And my neighbor? The real Sophie? She is sending off her applications and will be accepted and will go to college, and that series of actions will seem right if only because to me they are more familiar, linear, and measurable than the path my own daughter has chosen. But despite all our hopes and dreams and ministrations and writing of essays, children will become what they need to become.

Who is *my* real daughter? Can I see her clearly? Or can I only see what I hope for her? What is the right of an individual to the design of her life? When is it appropriate to step in? What is the difference between magical thinking and optimism? Between reality buoyed by reasonable ambition and fantasy? When is the tundra so fragile that any parental trespass is damaging? How can we know this about our children? Their vulnerability? How can we protect them, help them, and how long is that our responsibility? And when it no longer is, how can we stop?

T-minus Thirteen Minutes and Forty-one Seconds

. . . .

Steve Thomas

$\mathcal{D}$irecting a child through the college search requires metaphoric guidance. As a director of admissions at a highly selective liberal arts college, I am always looking for ways to communicate this delicate and dicey dance to parents. My inspiration for the ideal analogy came, quite unexpectedly, when I learned of Walter Cronkite's death. I remember him well from the years when he reported the world's happenings every night on my television screen. News of his passing transported me back to a time when he was present in my New Jersey grade school classroom in the early 1960s.

President Kennedy and NASA had decided to launch the Mercury space missions, partially in response to Russia's Sputnik program. The first missions were designed to escape Earth's gravity and return. Later missions were designed to orbit the Earth and to investigate the effect of such activity, first on chimpanzees and then on human beings. These were, of course, forerunners to the Gemini and Apollo programs that would successfully land a man on the moon in July 1969.

About the same time that NASA was launching its attack on space, my classmates and I perfected the art of hiding a transistor radio in a pants pocket and sneakily running the headphone wire under a long-sleeve shirt and then up the sleeve so that one could appear to casually lean one's ear on the palm of one's hand, containing the earpiece. We did this in October, when the Yankees were usually in the World Series. They played exclusively during the daylight hours back then and so we listened clandestinely and reported the score using hand signals when our classroom teacher had his back to us. Nowadays, I suspect students would just check their BlackBerries for the score and text their classmates the information from their pockets, no wires necessary.

When my fifth-grade teacher, Mr. Miller, wheeled the television set into my classroom for the first Mercury launch, it dawned on me that it would be technologically, though probably not politically, possible to watch the World Series games in class. Now, this was a radical discovery! But that's not what Mr. Miller had in mind. "Today's launch of the Mercury spacecraft with astronaut Alan Shepard aboard will be historic," said Mr. Miller. "As a class, we will watch on television in order to witness together this amazing event."

Seemed like a good idea to me. Launching a human into space hadn't been done before; so this event held the same unknown outcome as baseball games and other live sporting events. And as we watched the giant capsule, in black and white and shades of gray only, sit upon the launchpad at someplace called Cape Canaveral, we heard the cadence that was to become so familiar to all launches thereafter—the interminable countdown that always, at some time, for some reason or another, came to a stop.

"T-minus thirteen minutes and forty-one seconds and holding," Walter Cronkite would report in his stone voice of reassurance. And during the holding, as filler, we watched the earlier taped shot of the astronaut walking to and entering the space capsule. On his walk, the astronaut appeared to be lugging along a portable heater. Later, we learned he was carrying an important source of oxygen. After a minor check was performed on an obscure gauge that seemed out of whack to one of the launch specialists, the countdown resumed.

"T-minus nine minutes and counting," Walter crooned in his familiar authoritative voice.

Vapors from the liquid oxygen surrounded the bottom of the Redstone rocket and the tethered cords from the space capsule hung down, connected to Ground Control. I have to admit, it all seemed rather fantastical to me and quite unlikely to work. How could this all be integrated—the fuel, the machinery, the logistics, the power, the unknown—to escape Earth's gravity successfully? How could Shepard or Grissom or Glenn keep his cool during all that G-force thrust? It seemed damn implausible, and yet I watched with great attention, nearly as much attention as I gave to the Yankees games. Walter Cronkite's voice was the steady guarantee, the elixir of assurance, that all would work out well.

The countdown reached the one-minute mark and then slowly descended into seconds. We were glued to the images of the rocket, sitting there poised, steam billowing out beneath. I imagined the wives and the children of the astronauts at home, and the viewers sitting on the beaches miles away with their binoculars. Time slowed magically down.

And then, at last, the class chimed in with Walter. "Ten, nine, eight, seven, six, five, four, three ["Ignition," Walter inserted here], two, one, blast off . . ." The class, and I imagined the whole world, held its collective breath. "We have liftoff," Walter announced with a lilt, and we watched the giant spaceship begin to lift away from its launching pad. The screen appeared to shake as the platform equipment fell away. And then slowly, but surely, the giant Redstone rocket with the Mercury space capsule moved up into the sky and away from Earth's gravity. History was being made before our young eyes.

The post-launch coverage was different. As the behemoth moved away from the ground, the cameras focused on the rocket flame as it grew smaller and smaller. Mr. Cronkite was forced to fill in the relative lack of excitement on the screen with commentary and patter.

I'm not sure Mr. Miller or the folks who planned the television coverage ever really knew exactly what to do once the rocket moved higher into the sky. Their coverage at this time emulated political convention coverage when the mayor of a relatively unknown city was at the podium. There was a swell of "happy talk" and the beginning of the movement from one correspondent to another for another perspective. When exactly should the coverage end or should Mr. Miller turn off the television? This had never been decided conclusively by anyone. The launch coverage on television and in the classroom went on until the television cameras could barely pick up the image of the rocket in the sky.

Then there was this portentous moment, about eight or nine minutes into launch, that marked an important milestone of the journey and that seemed very important to Walter. About the same time that the giant Redstone would begin to escape Earth's gravity, we could see something separate from the capsule.

"There goes the booster rocket falling back to Earth."

This pronouncement by Walter has always stayed with me. It signified something good, something finally achieved—a kind of home run in the world of space travel. It wasn't until I became a director of admissions and had my own children that I realized what a fitting metaphor the whole rocket launch experience is, how it can serve as the perfect analogy for parenting a child through the college search process.

The child becomes the astronaut, headed to an unknown planet beyond the parental orbit; the college counselor acts as NASA Ground Control directing the launch and staying in constant communication. And parents are responsible for fulfilling one of the most critical roles of all—that of boosting the child into orbit.

Launching, propelling, and ultimately falling away isn't easy for parents, but choosing the right time to do so is, as Walter would have said, "mission critical." Once you have helped launch your child's college search—served as a chauffeur on those interminable college tours, created the spreadsheet of application deadlines, and proofed numerous essays—it's time to fall away and allow your children to escape the grip of your parental gravity. Now your son or daughter must drive the orbiter and assume the full responsibility for landing it on the right planet.

So as your sons and daughters receive their envelopes—the fat happy ones and the skinny disappointing ones—take a deep breath, parents. With your feet firmly planted on the Earth, breathe the richly oxygenated air. You've done everything you can do. You fueled their K–12 education and boosted them beyond the orbit of your family. The landing is now up to your son or daughter. Trust them to know which planet is right for them and to land the capsule successfully.

"And that's the way it is," Walter pronounced. Indeed.

About the Contributors

EMMA BRITZ graduated in 2008 from Kenyon College with a degree in international studies. She lives and works in Washington, D.C., and is embarking on the next step of the college search as she looks for a graduate school.

JAN BROGAN is an award-winning journalist and fiction writer. She is the author of *Teaser*, *Yesterday's Fatal*, *A Confidential Source*, and *Final Copy*, which won the Drood Review of Mystery's Editor's Choice Award.

SEAN CALLAWAY is the director of college placement and internships at the Center for Undergraduate Research Experiences of the Dyson College of Arts and Sciences where, since 1996, he supervises the college counseling of high school students in Pace University's federal and state programs. A graduate of the New York Studio School with a B.S. in studio art from SUNY Empire State College, Callaway is a father of six, grandfather of two, and can still walk without falling down.

JENNIFER DELAHUNTY has been the dean of admissions and financial aid at Kenyon College since 2003. Delahunty's articles and editorials have been published in *The New York Times*, *The Cleveland Plain Dealer*, the *National Association of College Admissions Counselors Journal*, and *The*

Lawlor Review. Her March 2006 Op-Ed, "To All the Girls I've Rejected," was widely syndicated by *The New York Times*. She attended Carleton College in Minnesota and the University of Arizona, from which she earned both her B.A. in history and an M.E.A. in creative nonfiction. Delahunty has parented two daughters through the college search process, both of whom chose colleges she would never have imagined.

LISA GATES, associate dean for planning and assessment and fellowships advisor at Middlebury College, has more than a decade of experience working with college students as an administrator and advisor. She has also taught courses on essay writing, German film, literature, and visual art, and has written about a diverse range of subjects, from ethnographic photography to raising children. The mother of three children, Gates received her B.A. from Dartmouth College and her Ph.D. from Harvard University.

JANE HAMILTON is the author of six award-winning novels. Her first novel, *The Book of Ruth*, won the PEN/Ernest Hemingway Foundation Award for best first novel and was a selection of the Oprah Book Club. Her second novel, *A Map of the World*, also selected for the Oprah Book Club, was an international bestseller. The mother of two college graduates, Jane lives, works, and writes in an orchard farmhouse in Wisconsin.

JOY HOROWITZ is a journalist and author whose work has appeared in *The New York Times*, the *Los Angeles Times*, and many other publications. Her most recent book, *Parts Per Million: The Poisoning of Beverly Hills High School*, was released in paperback by Viking in 2008.

GAIL HUDSON, a writer based in Seattle, has written

extensively about human relationships with family, community, animals, and the natural world. She is the co-editor of *I Wanna Be Sedated: 30 Writers on Parenting Teenagers*. Her most recent books include *Hope for Animals and Their World: How Endangered Species Are Being Rescued from the Brink* and *Harvest for Hope, A Guide to Mindful Eating*, both of which she wrote with Dr. Jane Goodall. Her personal essays have appeared in numerous publications, including *Good Housekeeping*, *Parents*, *Child*, *Natural Health*, *Utne Reader*, and *Self*. Gail is currently in the throes of guiding her youngest child through the college application process. So far he managed to get his University of California application submitted online fifty-five minutes before the December 1 deadline. She anticipates a long winter.

SARAH KAHRL is vice president for college relations at Kenyon College and has had a thirty-year career in fundraising for education and the arts. She learned the fundamentals of supervising a diverse group of forty-five fundraising professionals from her experience as a mother of four children whose aspirations range from evolutionary biology and wildlife management to becoming a big-city chef. Kahrl is a graduate of Smith College in theater and English literature.

LAURIE KUTCHINS is the author of three books of poems: *Slope of the Child Everlasting*, *The Night Path*, and *Between Towns*. *The Night Path* received the Isabella Gardner Award and was a Pulitzer nomination for Poetry in 1997. Her poems have appeared widely in anthologies and periodicals, including *The New Yorker*, *The Kenyon Review*, *Poetry*, *Ploughshares*, *Orion*, *The Georgia Review*, *The Southern Review*, *West Branch*, and other places. Her nonfiction has been published in *The Georgia Review*, *LIT*, *Urthona*, and in the anthologies *A Place on Earth: Nature Writing from Australia and North America*, *Woven on the Wind*, and *Let There Be Night*. Kutchins teaches creative writing at James Madison University in the Shenandoah Valley of Virginia. Her son is thriving as a "first-year" at the University of Virginia, and her daughter is in sixth grade.

DAN LASKIN is a writer and editor in the Office of Public Affairs at Kenyon College. In addition to working on the alumni magazine and a range of other Kenyon publications—including admissions literature—he writes a popular column, "Soundings," for the college's faculty-staff newsletter. A graduate of Yale University, Dan has been a newspaper reporter, a magazine editor, and a freelance writer. He travels frequently in France, thanks to his wife, Mary Jane Cowles, who teaches French at Kenyon. They have two sons, Gregory and Alexander.

DAVID LATT has a Ph.D. in seventeenth-century English literature from UCLA, taught college in California and Rhode Island, and is currently a television writer-producer, having worked for twenty-five years in Hollywood on shows as various as *Hill Street Blues* (for which he won an Emmy), *The Hitchhiker*, *Bakersfield P.D.*, *Get a Life*, *EZ Streets*, *Stir Crazy*, *Twin Peaks* (nominated for a second Emmy), and many others. He has co-written half a dozen pilot scripts and headed the writing staff of DotComix, a motion-capture animation Web site. He's also the author of the blog "Men Who Like to Cook" (www.menwholiketocook.blogspot.com), the happily married husband to Michelle, and the proud father of two sons, Franklin and Michael.

DAVID H. LYNN is the editor of *The Kenyon Review* and a professor of English at Kenyon College. His most recent book is *Year of Fire*, a collection of stories published by Harcourt. He is the father of Aaron and Elizabeth, and he is married to Wendy Singer, a historian of India.

WENDY MACLEOD is the James E. Michael Playwright-in-Residence at Kenyon College and author of such plays as *Juvenilia*, *Sin*, and *The Water Children*. Her plays have been produced at the Gate Theater in London, Steppenwolf and the Goodman in Chicago, and off-Broadway at Playwrights Horizons. Her play *The House of Yes* is a Miramax film starring Parker Posey. Her prose has been published in the *International Herald Tribune*, *The Washington Post*, *Poetry* magazine, and in the online culture journal therumpus.net.

THE NEUROTIC PARENT grew up in a northeastern metropolis, where mostly everybody was anxiety-ridden. She received her B.A. and M.A. from a large, public university. Later, after living in a developing country, she dropped out of a Ph.D. program in a fascinating yet impractical area of study. After working as a college instructor for four years, she managed to snag a job in the entertainment business, and won an Emmy in 2002. She is married to a classical musician who forces her to continue to write for television in order to afford their younger son's SAT tutor. She is currently adapting her blog, www.theneuroticparent.com, into a Broadway musical.

NEAL POLLACK has written four books: *Alternadad*, *Never Mind The Pollacks*, *The Neal Pollack Anthology of American Literature*, and *Beneath the Axis of Evil*. Pollack is also the editor of *Chicago Noir*, a collection of crime stories published by Akashic

Books. His next book, *STRETCH: The Unlikely Making of a Yoga Dude*, will be published in 2010 by Harper Perennial. He lives in Los Angeles with his wife and son.

JOE QUEENAN is the author of nine books and a regular contributor to *The New York Times*. His memoir *Closing Time* was published by Viking in 2009. It was a *New York Times* Notable Book of 2009, and was also selected one of the top books of the year by *The Washington Post*. His writing has been featured in *Time*, *Newsweek*, *GQ*, *Esquire*, *People*, *Forbes*, and *Rolling Stone*, among others. He is a frequent guest on network talk shows and has hosted radio programs for the BBC. A native of Philadelphia, he is married, with two children, and lives in Tarrytown, New York.

ANNA QUINDLEN's work has appeared in some of America's most influential newspapers, many of its best-known magazines, and on both fiction and nonfiction bestseller lists. She is a novelist and also writes the "Last Word" column in *Newsweek* magazine. A columnist at *The New York Times* from 1981 to 1994, in 1990 Quindlen became only the third woman in the paper's history to write a regular column for its influential Op-Ed page when she began the nationally syndicated "Public and Private." In 1992 Quindlen won the Pulitzer Prize for Commentary. In 1995 Quindlen left the world of newspapers, which she had joined as a copy girl at age eighteen, to become a novelist full time. Quindlen has written four bestselling novels: *Object Lessons*, *One True Thing*, *Black and Blue*, and *Blessings*. With the release of *A Short Guide to a Happy Life*, Quindlen became the first writer ever to have books appear on the fiction, nonfiction, and self-help *New York Times* bestseller lists.

ANNA DUKE REACH is director of programs for *The Kenyon Review*. Once upon a time, she attended Colgate University and worked in publishing for George Braziller and the Metropolitan Museum of Art. She is a mother of three beloved children who booked all her vacation time on college campuses for the past seven years. This year, she plans to stay home and read stories instead.

ANNE C. ROARK is a freelance writer in Los Angeles who spent over a decade covering healthcare and higher education for the *Los Angeles Times*. She is a contributing writer to the *New York Times* online blog "The New Old Age" (http://newoldage.blogs.nytimes.com/author/anne-c-roark/), has created two online blogs—"The Good Patient: Getting Better" and "Not on Call"—taught journalism courses at UCLA, and covered the politics of science and education for *The Chronicle of Higher Education* in Washington, D.C. Her articles have appeared in *Science*, *Psychology Today*, *Le Monde*, *The Washington Post*, *The Boston Globe*, *Chicago Tribune*, to name a few. Before becoming a reporter, Roark spent two years on the other side of the admissions process as an assistant director of admissions at her alma mater, Goucher College. For the past twenty-five years, she has been married to Marshall Goldberg, a film, television, and novel writer; Harvard graduate; and father of Kate and Rachel.

S. X. ROSENSTOCK is the author of *United Artists: Poems*, and a contributor to *By Herself: Women Reclaim Poetry* and *The Paris Review Book of Heartbreak, Madness, Sex, Love . . . Since 1953*. She is finishing a novel and lives in Los Angeles.

SCOTT SADIL writes and teaches in Hood River, Oregon. His fiction, essays, and articles appear regularly in the outdoor press. His books include the memoir *Angling Baja*, the novel *Cast from the Edge*, and a collection of fiction, *Lost in Wyoming*. A compilation of recent fly-fishing essays, *Fly Tales*, was published in 2010 by Barclay Creek Press.

DEBRA SHAVER has been in college admissions for over twenty-five years and has been the director of admissions at Smith College since 2003. She cites her experience as a parent guiding her son through the college process as her best professional development training. Shaver has spoken nationally about college admissions and has been recognized as a dynamic and humorous speaker on the role of parents in the college admission process. She received a bachelor's degree from Cornell University and a master's degree from Alfred University.

KATHERINE SILLIN has spent many years in independent schools and is currently the director of college counseling at North Yarmouth Academy in Yarmouth, Maine. Katherine graduated with a B.A. from Williams College and spent a year studying at Exeter College, Oxford University. She has two children who are far too young for the madness of this crazy process but who are exceedingly patient when family road trips involve peeling off the highway so Mom can quickly visit one college or another. Sillin enjoys writing— everything from college recommendations to short stories, to a novel currently in progress.

STEVE THOMAS is the director of admissions at Colby College, Waterville, Maine, and has worked as a teacher and administrator in both independent schools and colleges for his entire professional career. Thomas speaks frequently to students and parents around the country about the college search and is often quoted in the national press. He earned his bachelor's degree from North Carolina State University and a master's degree from Wesleyan University. He is raising two daughters on the shores of the Damariscotta River in Maine.

CHRISTINE VANDEVELDE is a writer whose work has appeared in newspapers, including *USA Today*, the *Chicago Tribune*, the *Los Angeles Times*, the *San Jose Mercury News*, and the *San Francisco Chronicle*, and national and regional magazines, such as *Self*, *Parenting*, *Home & Design*, and *Chicago*. She is currently coauthoring a book on college admissions with Robin Mamlet, the former dean of admissions at Stanford University, to be published by Three Rivers Press in 2011. Her daughter is completing her sophomore year at Vanderbilt University.

ELLEN WATERSTON is a published poet, as well as a nonfiction and fiction writer, living in Bend, Oregon. Her memoir, *Then There Was No Mountain*, was named one of the top ten books in 2003 by the *Oregonian* and was a *Foreword* and WILLA finalist. Her collection of poetry, *I Am Madagascar*, was awarded the WILLA Prize in Poetry in 2005. *Where the Crooked River Rises*, a collection of personal and nature essays, will be published in fall 2010 by Oregon State University Press. She is the mother of three adult children.

LISA K. WINKLER is an educator and a writer living in Summit, New Jersey. She holds a B.A. from Vassar College and an M.A. from New Jersey City University and is the mother of three children.

Copyright Acknowledgments

1. Univ of Chicago
2. Yale
3. Johns Hopkins
4. Harvard
5. Brown
6. Columbia

7. Brandeis
8. U of R
9. Penn
10. Cornell
11. ? Michigan
12. ? Wisconsin